A BASIC CATECHISM
Of The Christian Faith

By the same author:

Satan's Strategy, God's Remedy (evangelistic booklet)

Tongues, Prophecy, Healings...: An exposition of 1 Cor. 12-14 and related passages

The Hidden Life: A call to discipleship

The Keys of the Kingdom: A study on the biblical form of church government

The Rose of Sharon, the Lily of the Valleys: An Exposition on the Song of Solomon

A Garden Enclosed: A historical study and evaluation of the form of church government practised by the Particular Baptists in the 17th and 18th centuries.

A BASIC CATECHISM
Of The Christian Faith

B S POH

Published by Good News Enterprise

A BASIC CATECHISM OF THE CHRISTIAN FAITH

Copyright ©Boon-Sing Poh, 2013

ISBN: 978-983-9180-21-3

First published: 2013

This edition: March 2014 (A sharper font is used, and typos have been corrected.)

Published by:

GOOD NEWS ENTERPRISE, 52 Jalan SS 21/2,
Damansara Utama, 47400 Petaling Jaya, Malaysia.

www.rbcm.net; www.ghmag.net

Printed by:

CreateSpace, an Amazon company, United States of America.

Typeset by the author using TeXworks, the memoir class.

Dedicated to:

Yeh Han

Yeh Tze

Yeh Chuin

& Yeh Ern

"Behold, children *are* a heritage from the LORD."

(Psalm 127:3)

Contents

Preface ix

An Introduction xi

I THE GOSPEL 1

1 MAN, GOD, SCRIPTURE 3

2 WHAT GOD IS 9

3 WHAT GOD HAS DONE 15

4 HOW MAN SINNED 23

5 CHRIST THE REDEEMER 31

6 THE WORK OF CHRIST IN SALVATION 37

7 THE SPIRIT'S WORK IN SALVATION 45

8 THE BENEFITS OF SALVATION IN THIS LIFE 51

9 THE BENEFITS OF SALVATION AT DEATH 59

II THE LAW OF GOD 65

10 THE MORAL LAW 67

11 THE WORSHIP OF GOD	73
12 THE PRESERVATION OF THE FAMILY	83
13 THE PRESERVATION OF SOCIETY	89
14 THE PENALTY OF THE LAW	95
III THE CHRISTIAN LIFE	**99**
15 THE WAY TO BE SAVED	101
16 THE MEANS OF GRACE	109
17 THE SPECIAL ORDINANCES	117
18 GOD-CENTRED PRAYER	127
19 PRAYING FOR NEEDS	135
20 THE KINGDOM OF GOD	143
INDEX	161

Preface

This is a basic catechism (or ABC) of the Christian faith from the Reformed Baptist perspective. While there is no necessity to apologize for articulating one's faith, it is a matter of courtesy to brethren of other communions to inform them of this fact from the outset. This will also help those seeking to know the Christian faith to be aware that there are differences between Christians on some non-fundamental issues. The Reformed Baptists are known for their desire to uphold consistently the Reformation principles of *sola scriptura* (Scripture alone) and *semper reformanda* (always being reformed). This Catechism should be appreciated from this perspective, namely, the desire to submit ourselves to the authority of Scripture in doctrine and in practice.

Catechizing was known to be a practice of churches from apostolic time up to the Reformation. Among Protestants, only confessional churches of the Reformed tradition continue to value the use of catechisms, while the churches founded after the Reformation, such as the Brethren, Evangelical Free, and Methodist churches, do not use catechisms or confessions of faith. Sadly, many of the older churches that have their roots in the Reformation have also forsaken the use of such documents. The "no creed but the Bible" approach to the Christian life of the non-confessional churches has left them without an adequate tool to evangelize and to build up the faith of new believers. This, together with their accommodative spirit, has led them to embrace wholesale "the Alpha Course", produced by an Anglican church in London, which is Arminian in soteriology and Charismatic in outlook. The Church of England, of course, has for long relegated their traditional Thirty-nine Articles to a place of no practical importance.

This revised version of Keach's Catechism, produced by the Particular Baptists of the 17th century, takes into account the various revised editions produced in the past, including that of C. H. Spurgeon in the 19th century and others in recent days. Being a revision, the contents and structure remain basically the same as the original, with changes made in the wording and sentence construction to improve on readability for today. The division of the contents into sections will be helpful to readers, teachers, and students. The last section constitutes the most significant rearrangement, subsuming the doctrine of the church under the kingdom of God while adding new material on missions, the form of church government, and the end time.

This writer acknowledges with thanks the use of quotations from the New King James version of the Bible, published by Thomas Nelson, Inc. The members of the Damansara Reformed Baptist Church (DRBC) have been the anvil upon which the substance of this book was forged. His dear wife, Goody, has borne up with the neglect from a husband who spent many hours glued to the computer. Many friends have prayed for the ministry of this unworthy sinner saved by God's grace.

It is hoped that this Catechism, with the comments, will be well-used by Reformed Baptist churches, and that it will draw other churches to closer conformity to the Bible's teaching. This Catechism should be used alongside the opened Bible – in Sunday Schools, in house-to-house outreach, in Christian homes, in student outreach, in Bible Study groups, and in follow-up with new believers. May Christ have dominion "from sea to sea, and from the River to the ends of the earth" (Psalm 72:8). Amen.

BS Poh, May 2013

An Introduction

Systematic instruction in God's word is important to our spiritual growth and doctrinal stability. One ancient and proven way of instructing Christians in the doctrine of the Bible is by the method of catechizing, i.e. by asking questions and providing the answers.

The regular and systematic instruction of God's word appeared to have been developed by the time the book of Galatians was written (around AD 49). Galatians 6:6 says, "Let him who is taught the word share in all good things with him who teaches." The words "taught" and "teaches" are derived from "katecheo", to instruct. Theophilus appeared to have been "instructed" in a systematic manner (Luke 1:3-4).

Furthermore, Jude refers to "the faith" (v. 3), while Paul refers to "one faith" (Eph. 4:5), and "the whole counsel of God" (Acts 20:27 cf. 20-21), which is able to "build up" the believers (Acts 20:32; Jude 20 cf. 2 Pet. 3:18; Matt. 28:18-20). The Christian faith was definable, being made up of doctrines that were used to build up the spiritual life of the believers. The systematic instruction in biblical doctrines developed into the question-and-answer method known as "catechizing". The compiled doctrines in the question-and-answer approach became known as a "catechism".

History of the use of catechisms

After the apostles, catechizing became a chief means of instruction in the churches. It was used by the Roman Catholic Church and the Orthodox Churches to prepare "catechumens" for baptism. The Reformers used this as a means of instructing families. The catechism must be distinguished from other church documents.

Historically, three types of documents have been used by churches: (i) *creeds*, which are short statements of faith produced by the church councils in the first three hundred years after the apostles; (ii) *catechisms*, which are longer than creeds, couched as questions and answers, and used in baptismal classes and families; (iii) *confessions of faith*, which are longer than creeds and catechisms, and are used by Reformed churches to declare the doctrine held by the church.

Apart from being used as instructional tools, these documents served different purposes. The creeds (such as the Nicene Creed, the Apostles' Creed, and the Athanasian Creed) distinguish professing Christians from the followers of other faiths. They were produced by the "ecumenical councils" to defend the truth against errors. (These "ecumenical councils" must not be confused with the modern ecumenical movement, which seeks unity among churches at the expense of truth.) However, being too brief, the creeds do not help to distinguish between the Roman Catholic Church and the Protestant churches. The differences in belief between the churches show up in their respective catechisms and confessions of faith. Catechisms are intended to establish the faith of individual Christians, while the confessions of faith define the doctrine of a church.

Churches and denominations that were founded after the Reformation (e.g. Methodist, Brethren, Evangelical Free, etc.) do not use catechisms and confessions of faith. Such churches would generally accede to the creeds, and have a brief statement of faith, consisting of ten or fifteen articles, at most. Today, most churches do not value the catechisms and confessions of faith and claim, instead, to hold to "no creed but the Bible". Among the Protestant churches, only those that are Reformed (in the sense that we mean) are serious about using catechisms and confessions of faith. Such are often referred to as "confessional churches". As pointed out above, the catechism is useful in establishing the faith of the individual believers, while the confession of faith is useful in defining the beliefs of the church. In addition to the confession of faith, a Reformed church may adopt a statement of faith of, say, twelve articles to show visitors that it is a true (or evangelical) church. Reformed Baptist churches are generally confessional. How did this come about?

The Reformation began in 1517, when Martin Luther nailed his "Ninety-five Theses" to the door of the church at Wittenburg, Germany. The Reformation spread throughout Europe and Britain. By

An Introduction

1630, two groups of Baptists emerged in England – the General Baptists and the Particular Baptists. The heirs of the Particular Baptists are today called Reformed Baptists. The Baptists were persecuted by the government and the Church of England for most of the time. In 1677, a confession of faith was drawn up by the Particular Baptists, based on the Westminster Confession of the Presbyterians and the Savoy Declaration of the Congregationalists, to show their commitment to the same basic Reformed theology, although differing in baptism and church government. When toleration was granted in 1688, the confession of faith was published a year later which became known as the 1689 Baptist Confession of Faith.

In 1693, the Particular Baptists assigned William Collins to draw up a catechism. Based on the Westminster Shorter Catechism of the Presbyterians, a catechism was soon produced. Due to the involvement of another pastor, Benjamin Keach, who probably published and distributed it, the catechism became known widely as Keach's Catechism. Other catechisms have been produced over the years, but Keach's Catechism remains the most well-known and popular.

Structure of the catechism

Keach's Catechism (KC) follows closely the Westminster Shorter Catechism (WSC), in structure and content. The WSC has 107 questions while KC has 118. KC expands on the number of introductory questions from 3 to 7, adds two questions to the first division on the death and judgement of the wicked (Qs. 43 & 44), adds one question on the purpose of the law (Q. 89), alters and reduces the number of questions on the "sacraments" to two instead of three (Qs. 98 & 99), alters and adds three questions on baptism (Qs. 100-104), and adds two questions on the church (Qs. 105 & 106).

In 1855, C. H. Spurgeon published the catechism with just 82 questions, by reducing the number of questions on the Ten Commandments and leaving out totally the section on the Lord's Prayer. It seems that he modeled his version of the catechism after Thomas Watson's book, "A Body of Divinity", which did not include the Lord's Prayer. Watson produced a separate book of exposition on the Lord's Prayer. Spurgeon spoke highly of Watson's book, and republished it, but with an appendix written by himself, giving the Baptist view on baptism.

In recent days, "The Shorter Catechism: A Baptist Version" (SCBV) was produced by a group of Reformed Baptists in America, published by Simpson Publishing Company, which consists of 115 questions. The doctrine of the church in Keach's Catechism (Qs. 104 & 106) is left out, while alterations and additions are made to the doctrine of salvation (Qs. 88, 89, 93 & 94). The doctrine on Scripture is strengthened by an additional question (Q. 3).

The present Catechism is based on Keach's Catechism (KC), with reference to SCBV, WSC, and Spurgeon's Catechism (SC), in which the questions and answers are made simpler. It has been felt for a long while that such a version of the Catechism is needed, while remaining sufficiently comprehensive. Children who have been taught a much simpler Children's Catechism have grown into their teenage years confused by learning a longer and complicated adult catechism. A version that bridges the gap between these two would be ideal to serve as the only version that needs to be learned, and even memorized.

The questions are classified under twenty sections, the headings of which show the progression in contents. These sections may be considered as consisting of three parts – Part I covering the gospel, i.e. the good news of salvation; Part II covering the law of God; and Part III covering the Christian life. In Part I, a person who is new to the Christian faith, such as is encountered in pagan situations, would be led through a comprehensive understanding of the necessity of "Jesus Christ and Him crucified" and the way of salvation "by grace, through faith, in Christ alone". In Part II, the person is brought to understand the demands and purpose of the law of God. In Part III, the person is confronted with the necessity of repentance and faith, and of living a transformed life. Throughout, the objective is to produce a catechism, with commentary, that is suitable for establishing the faith of believers, for teaching their children, and for convincing seekers of the Bible's system of doctrine.

Part I

THE GOSPEL

One

MAN, GOD, SCRIPTURE

Q1. What is the chief end of man?
A1. Man's chief end is to glorify God[1], and to enjoy him for ever[2].

1. 1 Cor. 10:31, Therefore, whether you eat or drink, or whatever you do, do all to the glory of God.

2. Ps. 73:25-26, Whom have I in heaven *but You*? And *there is* none upon earth *that* I desire besides You. My flesh and my heart fail; *but* God *is* the strength of my heart and my portion forever.

Comments

The "chief end" is the chief purpose for which we are made. The "end" of man, therefore, is more than the "objective" or "purpose" of man. Rather, it is the "purpose for which he is made", i.e. man is designed to fulfill a purpose. We are created by God to show forth His praise while on earth, and to live happily with Him in heaven. The parts of a machine work smoothly when they are in their respective places, and doing what they are meant to do. So also, man will be happy only when he submits himself to God, learns of His will, and obeys Him.

However, we know that many people want to live as they like instead of seeking to please God. Like nuts and bolts that are fitted in the wrong places, they grind along in life, causing harm and pain to themselves and to others. Over and above this, they are provoking God and incurring guilt upon themselves. Some people appear to be selfless, doing many acts of charity and showing concern for mankind and the environment. However, they are doing all these because of their own reasons, which are centred upon man.

Only a person who knows God, through faith in Jesus Christ, is capable of living a God-centred life. Only such a person can glorify God. "To glorify God" does not mean "adding glory to God", which is impossible because God is already perfect. Rather, it means to reflect or manifest His glory. A Christian glorifies God because he lives in accordance to His word, with the view of pleasing Him. Men are able to see the goodness of God in his life.

Q2. What rule has God given to direct us how we may glorify him?
A2.[1] The word of God, namely the Scriptures of the Old and New Testaments[1,2], is the only rule to direct us how we may glorify and enjoy Him[3,4].

1 Eph. 2:20, *Having been built on the foundation of the apostles and prophets, Jesus Christ Himself being the chief cornerstone.*

2 2 Tim. 3:16-17, *All Scripture is given by inspiration of God, and is profitable for doctrine, for reproof, for correction, for instruction in righteousness, that the man of God may be complete, thoroughly equipped for every good work.*

3 Acts 17:11, *These were more fair-minded than those in Thessalonica, in that they received the word with all readiness, and searched the Scriptures daily to find out whether these things were so.*

4 1 John 1:3, *That which we have seen and heard we declare to you, that you also may have fellowship with us; and truly our fellowship is with the Father and with His Son Jesus Christ.*

---

[1]Instead of the original wordings, "The word of God, which is contained in the Scriptures of the Old and New Testament ..." we have dropped the expression, "which is contained" because of the wrong views of Liberalism and Barthianism.

1. MAN, GOD, SCRIPTURE

Comments

God speaks to us today by His word, the Bible. He no longer speaks by voices, dreams, or visions (Heb. 1:1; 2 Tim. 3:16-17). It is better to say, "The Bible says ..." or "God says in His word ..." rather than, "God spoke to me ..." as though direct revelation has been given to you personally. The Holy Spirit who inspired the writing of the Bible is the same Spirit who causes sinners to be born again. It is not surprising, therefore, that the Holy Spirit communicates God's will to His people by applying the Bible's teaching to them. The more we understand the Bible's teaching, the easier it is for us to make decisions in life.

The Bible consists of 39 books in the Old Testament and 27 books in the New Testament. We reject the books called "the Apocrypha", which the Roman Catholic Church has added to the Bible. The Bible is God's perfect, or complete and sufficient, revelation to man. Adding anything to it is like adding poison to a glass of pure water. Similarly, we do not accept the so-called "revelations" or "holy books" of others as inspired writings of God. Both **Liberalism** and **Barthianism** claim that God's word is "contained" in the Bible in a sense different from the Reformed position. Liberalism holds to the view that some parts of the Bible are the words of man, introduced in the process of copying and transmission. Barthianism (after the theologian Karl Barth), also known as **Neo-orthodoxy** believes that the Bible is the word of man, and becomes God's word only when some parts of it "speaks" to the man, i.e. when it affects him in a deeply personal way.

The Bible alone should be our authority in all matters of faith and practice. This is the Reformation principle of "sola scriptura". God's word is sufficient to guide the individual Christian and the church in our service to Him. The Christian should not allow church traditions, personal preferences and man-made laws to dictate his faith and obedience to God. The church should not allow *traditions*, *pragmatism*, and *expediency* to nullify the sole authority of the Bible. Traditions are practices introduced by man that have been handed down. Pragmatism is the idea that what appears to work must be right, regardless of the underlying principles or the doctrinal implications. Expediency means doing what is convenient rather than what is morally right.

Q3.[2] **What do the Scriptures mainly teach?**
A3. The Scriptures mainly teach what man is to believe concerning God, and what duty God requires of man[1,2,3].

1 2 Tim. 1:13, Hold fast the pattern of sound words which you have heard from me, in faith and love which are in Christ Jesus.

2 Eccl. 12:13, Let us hear the conclusion of the whole matter: fear God and keep His commandments, for this is man's all.

3 Mic. 6:8, He has shown you, O man, what *is* good; and what does the LORD require of you but to do justly, to love mercy, and to walk humbly with your God?

Comments

In order to achieve the chief end of our life, we need to know God and His will, and we also need to do what He requires of us. It is simplistic to regard the various Protestant catechisms as consisting of two parts – the first part being those things we need to believe concerning God, and the second part being those things we need to do in obedience to God. The catechism is only a summary of the Bible's teaching. It is the totality of the Bible's teaching that must be believed, and what we are to believe includes those things we are required to do. As far as the catechism is concerned, it is better to consider it as consisting of three parts. One part of the catechism covers the *gospel*, i.e. the good news of salvation. This includes the knowledge of: (i) God, our Creator; (ii) man, the sinner; and (iii) salvation, in Jesus Christ. Another part of the catechism covers *the law of God*: (i) the moral demands of God upon His creatures: (ii) the good purposes of the law; and (iii) the consequences of our failure to keep the law. The third part covers *the Christian life*: (i) the necessity of responding to the gospel in repentance and faith; (ii) the means by which a believer's faith is sustained and nurtured; and (iii) the responsibility and privilege of serving God.

---

[2]The word "principally" has been changed to "mainly".

1. MAN, GOD, SCRIPTURE

There are many things that are not taught in the Bible, e.g. how a computer works, when the Republic of China was founded, what Jesus Christ looked like, etc. However, the Bible alone reveals the way of salvation to sinners, and builds up the faith of believers so that they are able to serve God well (2 Tim. 1:8-10; 1 Pet. 1:22-23). The catechism and the confession of faith do not possess any authority in themselves, unlike the Bible which is God's word. They are only tools to help us learn the Bible's teaching. They are useful because, in them, the doctrines of the Bible are laid down systematically.

The catechism is designed to help the individual Christian in his faith, while the confession of faith is designed to help the church in upholding the faith. The church is as strong as its members. It is not good enough to have able church leaders who make a stand for the truth. It would be good if the members are strong in the faith – knowing the doctrines of their faith, trusting God under all circumstances, and doing what they know to be true.

Two

WHAT GOD IS

Q4. What is God?
A4. God is Spirit[1] – infinite[2], eternal[3], and unchangeable[4] – in His being[5], wisdom, power[6], holiness[7], justice, goodness and truth[8].

1 John 4:24, God *is* Spirit, and those who worship Him must worship in spirit and truth.

2 Job 11:7-9, Can you search out the deep things of God? Can you find out the limits of the Almighty? They are higher than heaven—what can you do? Deeper than Sheol—what can you know? Their measure *is* longer than the earth and broader than the sea.

3 Psalm 90:2, Before the mountains were brought forth, or ever You had formed the earth and the world, even from everlasting to everlasting, You *are* God.

4 James 1:17, Every good gift and every perfect gift is from above, and comes down from the Father of lights, with whom there is no variation or shadow of turning.

5 Exodus 3:14, And God said to Moses, "I AM WHO I AM." And He said, "Thus you shall say to the children of Israel, 'I AM has sent me to you.'"

6 Psalm 147:5, Great *is* our Lord, and mighty in power; His understanding *is* infinite.

7 Rev. 4:8, *The* four living creatures, each having six wings, were full of eyes around and within. And they do not rest day or night, saying: "Holy, holy, holy, Lord God Almighty, Who was and is and is to come!"

8 Exodus 34:6-7, And the LORD passed before him and proclaimed, "The LORD, the LORD God, merciful and gracious, longsuffering, and abounding in goodness and truth, keeping mercy for thousands, forgiving iniquity and transgression and sin, by no means clearing *the guilty*, visiting the iniquity of the fathers upon the children and the children's children to the third and the fourth generation."

Comments

Since God is Spirit, we should not question His existence simply because we cannot see, touch, or weigh Him. We cannot see electricity, but we know it is there when the bulb lights up. **Atheism** claims that there is no God. **Agnosticism** claims that it is not possible to know the existence of God. Both are unreasonable since they fail to take into consideration the evidences around us, including: (i) the existence of the universe; (ii) the design and orderliness of the things and creatures that exist; and (iii) the revelation of Scriptures. Although God is Spirit, the Bible often represents Him with human qualities, e.g. Ex. 6:6; Num. 12:8; 2 Chron. 16:9. (This is called "anthropomorphism".)

God has certain incommunicable attributes, i.e. characteristics or qualities that cannot be passed on to man, namely His infinity (i.e. unlimited by space), eternity (i.e. unlimited by time), and immutability (i.e. unchangeable in essence). His other attributes are communicable to man, but remain infinite, eternal and unchangeable in Himself. When the Son of God took upon Himself perfect human nature, His divine nature remained unchanged. Apart from the attributes mentioned, are there other attributes of God? There are many other attributes of God, such as His mercy, longsuffering, and love, which are subsumed under the ones mentioned. The true God is the greatest and best of being!

2. WHAT GOD IS

Q5. Are there more Gods than one?
A5. There is but one only[1, 2], the living and true God[3].

1 Deut. 6:4, Hear, O Israel: The LORD our God, the LORD *is* one!

2 Isaiah 44:6, Thus says the LORD, the King of Israel, and his Redeemer, the LORD of hosts: 'I *am* the First and I *am* the Last; besides Me *there is* no God.'

3 Jer. 10:10, But the LORD *is* the true God; He is the living God and the everlasting King. At His wrath the earth will tremble, and the nations will not be able to endure His indignation.

Comments

There is a propensity in man to worship idols made by his own hands (Isa. 44:9-20). Man then projects, by his own imagination, superhuman qualities and actions upon these idols. He also worships certain objects and creatures, believing that they have superhuman abilities (Rom. 1:22-23, 25). The spirits that are supposed to dwell in these objects or creatures cannot be the good angels who serve the true God. If present, as often they are, these must be bad spirits, or demons (Matt. 8:28; Acts 19:13-16). Evil spirits may pretend to do good to man with the view of gaining his devotion and worship (1 Cor. 10:18-20).

The Bible forbids us representing the true God with images (Ex. 20:2-3), worshipping idols (1 Cor. 10:14; Gal. 4:8-9; 1 Thess. 1:9), and having fellowship with demons (1 Cor. 10:21-22; 2 Cor. 6:16). Christians should not represent Jesus Christ in pictures, even when teaching children the Bible, because: (i) He is truly God; (ii) He is the perfect Man who cannot be represented accurately by pictures; (iii) the Bible has not shown how He looked like (apart from Him being "a Man of sorrows and acquainted with grief" (Is. 53:3), and appearing older than His age (John 8:57)); (iv) true faith comes by hearing, not by sight (Rom. 10:17; John 20:29).

Q6. How many persons are there in the Godhead?
A6. There are three persons in the Godhead, the Father, the Son, and the Holy Spirit, and these three are one God[1], the same in substance, equal in power and glory[2,3].

1 Matt. 28:19, Go therefore and make disciples of all the nations, baptizing them in the name of the Father and of the Son and of the Holy Spirit.

2 2 Cor. 13:14, The grace of the Lord Jesus Christ, and the love of God, and the communion of the Holy Spirit *be* with you all. Amen.

3 1 John 5:7, For there are three that bear witness in heaven: the Father, the Word, and the Holy Spirit; and these three are one.

Comments

In the first 300 years after the apostles, the church was plagued with wrong teachings on the Godhead. There were those who claimed that the God of the New Testament is not the same as the God of the Old Testament, that the Father alone is the true God while Jesus Christ is the highest of His creatures, that Jesus Christ is not truly human or not truly divine, that the three Persons of the Godhead are not really equal, or that the three Persons are different modes of existence of the one God. The answer to this question of the catechism is a precise and concise statement of the true doctrine on the Trinity.

The Holy Spirit is divine and not a mere force, or power, or an influence. His role in God's work must be correctly recognized – in *regeneration* (John 3:5-8), *sanctification* (Rom 8:12-13; 1 Pet. 1:22-23), and *service to God* (Acts 4:8, 31). The Holy Spirit must not be separated from the word of God (Eph. 5:18-19 cf. Col. 3:16). Those who are truly filled with the Holy Spirit will be preaching God's word and focussing on the Lord Jesus Christ (John 14:26; Luke 24:44-48). The **Charismatic movement** wrongly emphasizes the role of the Holy Spirit at the expense of the word of God and the Lord Jesus Christ. They wrongly associate the work of the Holy Spirit with their claimed prophecies, healing and tongue-speaking. These miraculous gifts have been withdrawn by God after the completion of Scripture and the passing of the apostles (Rom. 15:18-19; 2 Cor. 12:12; Heb. 2:3-4).

Three

WHAT GOD HAS DONE

Q7. What are the decrees of God?
A7. The decrees of God are His eternal purpose, according to the counsel of His own will, whereby for His own glory, He has fore-ordained whatever comes to pass[1].

1 Eph. 1:11-12, In Him also we have obtained an inheritance, being predestined according to the purpose of Him who works all things according to the counsel of His will, that we who first trusted in Christ should be to the praise of His glory.

Comments

The plan of God has existed from eternity and will never change. This is different from chance or fate, for God is a living and intelligent being who powerfully controls all things, without suppressing the human will and the so-called laws of nature, created by Himself. Man, therefore, is not reduced to a mere robot or a pawn on a chessboard but is held responsible for his actions. Being good, holy and just, God is not the author of sin or evil. Rather, He allows these to happen while bringing them to fulfill His good and wise purpose.

Christians do not believe in "fate", "chance", or "luck". Christians do not consult mediums or the horoscope (of any kind, whether astrology, palmistry, etc.) to determine the future. Instead, they would trust in God, pray, and read the Bible. It is not appropriate for Christians to say, "I am lucky ...", or "Luckily..." It is more appropriate to say, "Thanks be to God ...", "Providentially ...", "Thankfully ...", "Happily ...", or some similar expressions that do not attribute events to "fate", "chance", or "luck".

Q8. How does God execute His decrees?
A8. God executes His decrees in the works of creation[1], and providence[2].

1 Rev. 4:11, You are worthy, O Lord, to receive glory and honor and power; for You created all things, and by Your will they exist and were created.

2 Dan. 4:35, All the inhabitants of the earth *are* reputed as nothing; He does according to His will in the army of heaven and *among* the inhabitants of the earth. No one can restrain His hand or say to Him, "What have You done?"

Comments

Creation concerns the origin of all things. *Providence* concerns actions and events seen in space and time (i.e. in the universe and throughout history). These are subjects too vast for man to handle, yet unbelieving people attempt to usurp God by giving alternative views of the origin of things and declaring their own sufficiency. Apart from folklores and religious beliefs, the so-called "theory of evolution" has influenced people throughout the world since the 19th century.

We derive great comfort from submitting ourselves to God, realizing that He is in absolute control, such that our life is filled with purpose, a sense of direction, and a sense of destiny. We have a duty to use our minds to think, and to act responsibly and righteously. At the same time, we are trusting in God who is in control, and who works out all things for His glory and the good of His people (James 4:13-17; Rom. 9:28).

3. WHAT GOD HAS DONE

Q9. What is the work of creation?
A9.[1] **The work of creation is God's making all things of nothing**[1]**, by the word of His power**[2]**, in six normal consecutive days**[3]**, and all very good**[4]**.**

1 Gen. 1:1, In the beginning God created the heavens and the earth.

2 Heb. 11:3, By faith we understand that the worlds were framed by the word of God, so that the things which are seen were not made of things which are visible.

3 Ex. 20:11, For *in* six days the LORD made the heavens and the earth, the sea, and all that *is* in them, and rested the seventh day. Therefore the LORD blessed the Sabbath day and hallowed it.

4 Gen. 1:31, Then God saw everything that He had made, and indeed *it was* very good. So the evening and the morning were the sixth day.

Comments

Man makes things out of existing things. He "creates" a piece of art, music, or architecture from concepts learned from existing things. Only God created all things out of nothing – including space, time, designs, objects, and life. He did so effortlessly, by His divine power. Everything was accomplished in six normal consecutive days, all according to His plan. Nothing was done too slowly or too fast. Everything created by God was very good – physiologically and morally. In other words, the end-product of creation did not show any deficiency in the power, wisdom, and holiness of God.

Two points must be noted. First, the alternative theories of the origin of things are contrary to the teaching of Scriptures – including **atheistic evolution, theistic evolution, the gap theory,** and **progressive (or process) creation.** Quite many Christians who reject atheistic evolution attempt to incorporate important aspects of

---

[1]We have adopted the wordings of C. H. Spurgeon, replacing "in the space of six days" with "in six normal consecutive days". Darwinism, i.e. the theory of evolution, was already a problem in Spurgeon's time.

the theory, including the idea that the earth is billions of years old, into the Bible's teaching on creation. Theistic evolutionists believe that God started the "Big Bang", and occasionally intervened, such as when He breathed into certain "pre-Adamic man" the breath of life. The gap theory claims that there was a gap of millions of years between the first two verses of Genesis 1, which is not recorded. Process creationists claim that the "day" in Genesis 1 is not a single rotation of the earth but a long undefined period of time. All these "theories" require that there was death, disease and suffering before the sin of Adam, that God did not create everything "very good", and assumes the earth is billions of years old.

Second, evil is not inherent in the creation of God, but in the sinful nature of fallen man. We must not think that material things are somehow evil while the soul of man is pure, and put the blame of our suffering upon the things and circumstances around us. A system of belief of the third century called **Gnosticism** teaches that the material body is evil while the soul is pure. It led to asceticism, i.e. the suppression of bodily appetites to promote spirituality.

Q10. What are God's works of providence?
A10.[2] God's works of providence are His powerful preserving[1] and governing all His creatures[2], and all events[3].

1 Heb. 1:3, Who being the brightness of *His* glory and the express image of His person, and upholding all things by the word of His power, when He had by Himself purged our sins, sat down at the right hand of the Majesty on high.

2 Ps. 103:19, The LORD has established His throne in heaven, and His kingdom rules over all.

3 Matt. 10:29, Are not two sparrows sold for a copper coin? And not one of them falls to the ground apart from your Father's will.

---

[2]We have replaced "His most holy, wise, and powerful..." with "His powerful...", believing that the emphasis intended lies there. God's attributes of holiness and wisdom have been included in Q4. Furthermore, "and all their actions" is redundant and has been replaced by "and all events", because events such as earthquakes and volcanic eruptions are also under God's control.

3. WHAT GOD HAS DONE

Comments

God did not create all things and then leave them to operate by in-built laws. Instead, all things – whether good or bad, big or small, done by man or occurring in nature – are maintained by His power and controlled by His will. Even the so-called laws of nature are under His control. As noted under Q7, Christians should avoid saying, "I was lucky", etc. Instead, we should say, "Thankfully...", "Happily...", "God was pleased to..." or "God saw fit to..."

Two things should be noted. Firstly, God is not the author or cause of evil. Christians may suffer in common with other people in this fallen world. God is in control of all things and has allowed even the bad events to happen, but that is different from saying He caused those bad events. Why He allows His people to be harmed and to suffer is a mystery. We can rest assured, however, that all things will work out for the good of His people, and to His glory (Rom. 8:28; Heb. 13:5). Secondly, Christians are held responsible for their actions (James 1:13-18). We must act responsibly and righteously while trusting in God who is in control (James 4:13-17). Those who plan for nothing gets nothing (Prov. 6:6-11).

Q11. How did God create man?
A11.[3] **God created man, male and female, after His own image**[1]**, in knowledge, holiness, and righteousness**[2, 3]**, with dominion over the creatures**[4]**.**

1 Gen. 1:27, So God created man in His *own* image; in the image of God He created him; male and female He created them.

2 Col. 3:10, And have put on the new man who is renewed in knowledge according to the image of Him who created him.

3 Eph. 4:24, And that you put on the new *man* which was created according to God, in true righteousness and holiness.

---

[3]Instead of "knowledge, righteousness, and holiness", the order has been changed to correspond to the normal orders of "mind, heart, and will" and "prophet, priest, and king".

4 Gen. 1:28, Then God blessed them, and God said to them, "Be fruitful and multiply; fill the earth and subdue it; have dominion over the fish of the sea, over the birds of the air, and over every living thing that moves on the earth."

Comments

God created woman to complement man. Any idea of the superiority of the one and the inferiority of the other is contrary to the teaching of the Bible (Gal. 3:27-28). Up to today, there are cultures that treat women as inferior to men. Any attempt to blur the distinction between male and female also is contrary to Scripture (1 Cor. 11:2-16). The modern feminist movement tends to do this while fighting for women's rights.

God created human beings to bear His image, i.e. with the ability to know spiritual truths, to worship God, and to obey His laws. Man is to act as prophet, priest and king – having dominion over the other creatures. It is man's responsibility to explore, to learn, to use, and to create. The whole of God's creation is for man to use, not to abuse (Gen. 1:28). Trees may be chopped down for use but the environment must not be destroyed through indiscriminate deforestation and greed. Those who engage in modern biological research are doing a noble work, but they must guard against abuse such as experimenting with, and destroying, human foetuses.

Q12.[4] What special act of providence was exercised toward man when he was created?
A12. When God had created man, He entered into a covenant of works with him, upon condition of perfect obedience; forbidding him to eat of the tree of the knowledge of good and evil, upon pain of death[1].

---

[4]We have replaced "in the estate wherein he was created" in the question with, "when he was created" to correspond with the answer which begins with, "When God had created man...". A semi-colon is used to separate the two parts of the answer.

3. WHAT GOD HAS DONE

1 Gen. 2:16-17, And the LORD God commanded the man, saying, "Of every tree of the garden you may freely eat; but of the tree of the knowledge of good and evil you shall not eat, for in the day that you eat of it you shall surely die."

Comments

Our Creator entered into a covenant, i.e. a formal agreement, with man based on the conditions He determined. This covenant of works required perfect obedience on the part of man. Adam was created with a free will, given the incentive to eat from all the other trees, and given the warning of the consequence of disobedience. It could not be said that God was unfair toward Adam.

If Adam had kept God's command, he would have continued to enjoy the blessed life of fellowship with God in the garden of Eden. This we know because he was allowed to eat from the tree of life before the Fall (Gen. 3:22 cf. Gen. 2:16). In fact, he might have been raised to an even higher level of existence. Adam, however, failed and came under God's judgement.

Four

HOW MAN SINNED

Q13.[1] Did our first parents continue in the state they were created?
A13. Our first parents, being left to the freedom of their own will, fell from the state they were created by eating the forbidden fruit[1], thereby sinning against God[2].

1 Gen. 3:6-8, So when the woman saw that the tree *was* good for food, that it *was* pleasant to the eyes, and a tree desirable to make *one* wise, she took of its fruit and ate. She also gave to her husband with her, and he ate. Then the eyes of both of them were opened, and they knew that they *were* naked; and they sewed fig leaves together and made themselves coverings. And they heard the sound of the LORD God walking in the garden in the cool of the day, and Adam and his wife hid themselves from the presence of the LORD God among the trees of the garden.

2 Eccl. 7:29, Truly, this only I have found: That God made man upright, but they have sought out many schemes.

---

[1]Following, C. H. Spurgeon, we have changed the old English word "estate" to "state" in both the question and the answer, and eliminated the question after the next, viz. "What is the sin whereby our first parents fell from the estate wherein they were created?" by bringing the answer into the present one.

Comments

Adam and Eve had free will in the sense that they had the *liberty* and *ability* to choose whether or not to obey God. Satan could tempt them, but he could not force them to act. The one command God gave them in the garden of Eden was not to eat of the tree of the knowledge of good and evil. The incentive for them to obey was that they could eat of the myriads of other trees. The warning against disobedience was that they would die. By disobeying God, they fell from the state of innocence into the state of sin. That first sin of Adam and Eve is often called the Fall.

Arminianism wrongly teaches that man has free will in the same way that Adam and Eve had. However, the Fall has caused man to lose the *ability* to choose what is pleasing to God, although he still retains the *liberty* of choice. Man's will is in bondage to his nature, which is now sinful.

Liberalism wrongly teaches that the story of the Fall is not factual, but a fable containing moral truths found in the experiences of man. Liberals, also known as **Modernists**, largely accept the teaching of evolution concerning the origin of man, and reject the authority of the Bible. The Lord Jesus Christ, however, accepted the account of the Fall as true (Matt. 19:4), and so did the apostle Paul (Rom. 5:12-21).

Q14. What is sin?
A14. **Sin is any lack of conformity to, or transgression of, the law of God**[1].

1 1 Jn. 3:4, Whoever commits sin also commits lawlessness, and sin is lawlessness.

Comments

There are *sins of omission*, i.e. the failure to do what is commanded by God. There are also *sins of commission*, i.e. the doing of what is forbidden by God. The law of God, whether given as one command to Adam and Eve, or as the Ten Commandments to the nation of

4. HOW MAN SINNED

Israel, or as the two great commandments by the Lord Jesus Christ, requires perfect obedience from man (James 2:10). This we have failed miserably to do (Gal. 3:10-12; Rom. 3:10).

Sin is defined in reference to the law of God. When defined in reference to man, it becomes *subjective*, i.e. based on one's feeling, and *relative*, i.e. different for different individuals. In the Fall, the devil shifted the focus from God's command to Eve's desire and choice (Gen. 3:4-5). Sin is primarily directed against God, and secondarily against man. We sin against man only because we have broken God's law, and therefore, offended God first. The prodigal son confessed, "Father, I have sinned against heaven and in your sight, and am no longer worthy to be called your son (Luke 15:21)." David confessed, "Against You, You only, have I sinned, and done *this* evil in Your sight—that You may be found just when You speak, *and* blameless when You judge."

Q15. Did all mankind fall in Adam's first transgression?
A15.[2] **All mankind descending from Adam by ordinary generation, sinned in him, and fell with him in his first transgression, because he was their representative in the covenant God made with man**[1,2].

1 Rom. 5:18, Therefore, as through one man's offense *judgment* came to all men, resulting in condemnation, even so through one Man's righteous act *the free gift came* to all men, resulting in justification of life.

2 1 Cor. 15:22, For as in Adam all die, even so in Christ all shall be made alive.

Comments

We have no choice in certain matters, e.g. the circumstances of our birth. God sovereignly determines such matters for us. He placed

---

[2]The clause, "The covenant being made with Adam, not only for himself but for his posterity," has been changed to "because he was their representative in the covenant God made with man," and moved to the end of the answer. That way, the answer is a direct response to the question, while the changed clause is subordinate.

Adam as the representative head of the human race. Just as a head of state acts on behalf of his country, Adam acted on behalf of the human race. When Adam sinned against God, the whole of mankind sinned in him. When Adam fell in his first transgression, the whole of mankind fell with him.

Unlike us, Jesus Christ did not descend from Adam by ordinary generation. Instead, He was conceived in the womb of Mary, and protected from sin, by the power of the Holy Spirit (Luke 1:35). He is sinless, although deriving His human nature from Mary (John 8:46; 2 Cor. 5:21).

Q16.[3] Into what state did the fall bring mankind?
A16. The fall brought mankind into a state of sin and misery[1].

1 Rom. 5:12, Therefore, just as through one man sin entered the world, and death through sin, and thus death spread to all men, because all sinned.

Comments

The Fall has consequences upon mankind. From the state of innocence and blessedness enjoyed by Adam and Eve before the Fall, mankind plunged into a state of sin and misery. Man's relationship with God is adversely affected, and his nature becomes sinful. The sinful nature in man affects him in his total personality – in mind, heart, and will.

The human race is one, descending from Adam and Eve. Unlike animals which are created in various species under different genera (singular, genus), the human race is just one species. Apart from superficial differences such as colour of skin, size of body, and facial features, we all share the same physical and biological makeup. The tallest and fairest Caucasian can marry the shortest and darkest African and produce healthy, normal, children. Similarly, we all share the same sinful nature, which inclines us to break God's law

---

[3] Again, the word "estate" has been changed to "state" in both the question and the answer.

4. HOW MAN SINNED

and to live by the desires of the flesh. Children in China grow up selfish and rebellious like children in America.

Q17.[4] What is the sinfulness of that state into which man fell?
A17. All mankind, by their fall, became guilty in Adam's first sin[1] and corrupt in their whole nature, which is commonly called original sin[2-4], leading to all actual transgressions[5].

1 Rom. 5:19, For as by one man's disobedience many were made sinners, so also by one Man's obedience many will be made righteous.

2 Rom. 3:10, As it is written: *"There is none righteous, no, not one."*

3 Eph. 2:1, And you *He made alive*, who were dead in trespasses and sins.

4 Ps. 51:5, Behold, I was brought forth in iniquity, and in sin my mother conceived me.

5 Matt. 15:19, For out of the heart proceed evil thoughts, murders, adulteries, fornications, thefts, false witness, blasphemies.

Comments

Man, in his sinful state, is faced with two problems – first, that of guilt due to Adam's sin, and second, that of a corrupt nature transmitted down from Adam and Eve. The corrupt nature in man inclines him to break God's law so that he becomes guilty of his own acts of sin.

This does not mean that man is as sinful as he possibly can be, nor is he as sinful as those in hell or the devil. The *degree* of sin must be distinguished from the *extent* of sin. Man is corrupt in his

---

[4]This question has been simplified to correspond with the form of the next, both of which are intended to elucidate the answer of Q15. The answer leaves out "the want of original righteousness" since that is stated in another way in the next phrase, "corrupt in their whole nature". Also, the closing clause, "together with all actual transgressions which proceed from it" has been tidied up.

whole nature, not just in some parts of it. This has been called "Total Depravity". This means that man is incapable of pleasing God in anything, unless his two problems are solved in some ways.

Q18. What is the misery of that state into which man fell?
A18. All mankind, by their fall, lost communion with God[1], are under His wrath and curse[2,3], and so made liable to all the miseries in this life, to death itself, and to the pains of hell for ever[4,5].

1 Gen. 3:8, 24, And they heard the sound of the LORD God walking in the garden in the cool of the day, and Adam and his wife hid themselves from the presence of the LORD God among the trees of the garden. So He drove out the man; and He placed cherubim at the east of the garden of Eden, and a flaming sword which turned every way, to guard the way to the tree of life.

2 Eph. 2:3, Among whom also we all once conducted ourselves in the lusts of our flesh, fulfilling the desires of the flesh and of the mind, and were by nature children of wrath, just as the others.

3 Gal. 3:10, For as many as are of the works of the law are under the curse; for it is written, *"Cursed is everyone who does not continue in all things which are written in the book of the law, to do them."*

4 Rom. 6:23, For the wages of sin *is* death, but the gift of God *is* eternal life in Christ Jesus our Lord.

5 Matt. 25:41, Then He will also say to those on the left hand, 'Depart from Me, you cursed, into the everlasting fire prepared for the devil and his angels.'

Comments

The *immediate* effects of the Fall upon mankind are that they lost the blessed fellowship with God and came under His wrath and curse. The *life-long* effects are that they become exposed to the pain and sufferings brought about by sin, including death itself. The *everlasting* effect is that they will experience the pains of hell, first in their souls, and after the judgement, in their souls and bodies together.

Annihilationism teaches that the souls of the wicked will gradually cease to exist (annihilated) while being punished in hell. The Bible's teaching is that there is everlasting punishment in hell for the wicked, whose destiny is irrevocably sealed at death. In other words, there is no "second chance" to be reconciled with God after death.

Five

CHRIST THE REDEEMER

Q19. Did God leave all mankind to perish in the state of sin and misery?
A19. God having, out of His good pleasure from all eternity[1], elected some to everlasting life[2], did enter into a covenant of grace[3] to deliver them out of the state of sin and misery, and to bring them into a state of salvation by a Redeemer[4].

1 Eph. 1:4, 9, Just as He chose us in Him before the foundation of the world, that we should be holy and without blame before Him in love ... having made known to us the mystery of His will, according to His good pleasure which He purposed in Himself.

2 2 Thess. 2:13, But we are bound to give thanks to God always for you, brethren beloved by the Lord, because God from the beginning chose you for salvation through sanctification by the Spirit and belief in the truth.

3 Gen. 3:15, And I will put enmity between you and the woman, and between your seed and her Seed; He shall bruise your head, and you shall bruise His heel.

4 2 Tim. 1:9, Who has saved *us* and called us with a holy calling, not according to our works, but according to His own purpose and grace which was given to us in Christ Jesus before time began.

Comments

Man is incapable of saving himself from the state of sin and misery. God, being all-knowing and all-merciful, has taken the initiative to save him. This involves the following: (i) God choosing certain people, and not all, to be saved; (ii) God making this choice from eternity, i.e. from before the creation of anything, including man; (iii) God making the choice based on His pleasure alone, since there is nothing good in man, nor in anything that he does; (iv) God entering into a covenant of grace with man after the Fall to save him through a Redeemer. This doctrine has been called "Unconditional Election".

Three common objections have been raised against the doctrine of Unconditional Election: (i) that God is unfair in arbitrarily choosing certain people while passing by others; (ii) that there may be some people who desire to be saved but are already predestined to be condemned; (iii) that those saved can live as they like, including sinning against God. Against these objections are: (i) God is our Creator and has every right to do what He wants (Rom. 9:14-21; Matt. 20:15); (ii) sinful people do not desire to be saved in God's way unless God first draws them (John 6:44, 65; Eph. 2:1-4); (iii) those saved would have a renewed nature and would not want to live in sin, although they are still not perfect while in this world (Rom. 6:15-19).

The *covenant of grace* contrasts with the *covenant of works*, in which man is obliged to keep the law of God perfectly in order to live. Unlike before the Fall, man is no more capable of keeping the law of God perfectly. Instead, he stands condemned by the law and, therefore, needs God's mercy to be saved. In the covenant of grace, God shows His mercy to unworthy sinners by providing a Redeemer for him. A Redeemer is needed because sinners cannot be forgiven without the penalty of their sins being paid for, and a righteousness found for him. In other words, the two problems he is faced with needs to be resolved, viz. his guilt before God and the corruption of his nature.

5. CHRIST THE REDEEMER

Q20. Who is the Redeemer of God's elect?
A20. The only Redeemer of God's elect is the Lord Jesus Christ[1], who being the eternal Son of God, became man[2], and so was and continues to be God and Man, in two distinct natures and one person for ever[3, 4].

1 1 Tim. 2:5-6, For *there is* one God and one Mediator between God and men, *the* Man Christ Jesus, who gave Himself a ransom for all, to be testified in due time.

2 John 1:14, And the Word became flesh and dwelt among us, and we beheld His glory, the glory as of the only begotten of the Father, full of grace and truth.

3 Rom. 9:5, Of whom *are* the fathers and from whom, according to the flesh, Christ *came*, who is over all, *the* eternally blessed God. Amen.

4 Col. 2:9, For in Him dwells all the fullness of the Godhead bodily.

Comments

The following must be noted about the salvation of sinners: (i) Jesus Christ is the only Redeemer. There is no other Saviour appointed by God to save sinners (Acts 4:2). This contradicts the universalistic view of salvation held by the **ecumenical movement**, which teaches that there is saving truth in all religions for those who are sincere and earnest. (ii) Christ, by His death on the cross, saves only the elect (Matt. 20:28; John 17:20; Rom. 5:10-11). This is the doctrine of "Particular Redemption". This is contradicted by **Arminianism** (after the Dutch theologian, James Arminius) and **Amyraldianism** (after French theologian, Moses Amyraut). Arminianism teaches a doctrine of Universal Atonement in which Christ died for everyone in the world, but only those who respond to the call of the gospel are saved. Amyraldianism teaches that Christ's death was "sufficient for all, and efficient for some". It stretches the *extent* of the atonement to include everyone, and restricts the *intent* of the atonement to the elect. This view was held by the 17th century Puritan, Richard Baxter, and by the 18th century Particular Baptist, Andrew Fuller.

Jesus Christ is not "half-God and half-Man". He is fully God and fully Man. He is one Person with two distinct natures – a divine nature which has existed from eternity and which remains unchanged, as well as a sinless but true human nature that came into existence when He was conceived in the womb of the virgin Mary by the power of the Holy Spirit. These two natures are inseparably united "without conversion, composition, or confusion" (1689 Confession, 8:2). In the past, there were those who believed that either Christ's divine nature became reduced so that He was not equal with the Father and the Spirit, or His human nature became enhanced so that He was not truly human. Others, like the **Jehovah's Witnesses** today, believed that the two natures of Christ became mixed so that a new nature midway between the two came into existence. Yet others believed that the two natures resulted in two persons, so that there were times when Christ appeared more like man, and other times when He appeared more like God. We must beware of believing in "another Jesus", different from the one taught in the Bible (2 Cor. 11:3-5).

The full title, "the Lord Jesus Christ" is appropriate because: (i) it describes well His role as Redeemer, for He is "Lord", i.e. Jehovah, and He is "Jesus", i.e. the Saviour, and He is "Christ", i.e. the anointed (or God-appointed) One; (ii) believers should show proper reverence to Him, as taught by the apostles (e.g. 2 Tim. 4:1, 22; 2 Pet. 1:8, 11, 16). Too many Christians today show an irreverent familiarity towards the Lord by referring to Him as "Jesus". As noted under Q5, we would not represent the Lord in pictures, even when teaching children the Bible. The reasons are: (i) since Jesus Christ is truly God, representing Him in pictures would be breaking the Second Commandment; (ii) since Jesus Christ is perfect Man, it would be impossible to present Him perfectly in pictures; (iii) no description of what the Lord looked like is given in the Bible; and (iv) true faith in Christ comes by hearing the word of God, not by seeing pictures of Him (Rom. 10:17; John 20:29).

5. CHRIST THE REDEEMER

Q21. How did Christ, being the Son of God, become man?
A21.[1] Christ, the son of God, became man by taking to Himself a true body[1], and a rational soul[2, 3], being conceived by the power of the Holy Spirit in the Virgin Mary, and born of her[4], yet without sin[5].

1 Heb. 2:14, Inasmuch then as the children have partaken of flesh and blood, He Himself likewise shared in the same, that through death He might destroy him who had the power of death, that is, the devil.

2 Matt. 26:38, Then He said to them, "My soul is exceedingly sorrowful, even to death. Stay here and watch with Me."

3 Heb. 4:15, For we do not have a High Priest who cannot sympathize with our weaknesses, but was in all *points* tempted as *we are, yet* without sin.

4 Luke 1:27, 31, 35, To a virgin betrothed to a man whose name was Joseph, of the house of David. The virgin's name *was* Mary. ... And behold, you will conceive in your womb and bring forth a Son, and shall call His name JESUS. ... And the angel answered and said to her, "*The* Holy Spirit will come upon you, and the power of the Highest will overshadow you; therefore, also, that Holy One who is to be born will be called the Son of God.

5 Heb. 7:26, For such a High Priest was fitting for us, *who is* holy, harmless, undefiled, separate from sinners, and has become higher than the heavens.

Comments

In the past, there were the **Docetists** who held that Christ only appeared to have a physical body, when He was actually a Spirit. Then, there were the **Arians** and **Eunomians**, who held that Christ received only human flesh, not human nature, from Mary, while the eternal Word took the place of the human soul. Another group called

---
[1]The word "reasonable" has been replaced by "rational".

the **Appollinarians** regarded man as consisting of three parts – the body, the sensible soul, and the rational soul. They believed that in Jesus Christ, the rational soul was replaced by the Word. The church leaders met at the **Council of Chalcedon** in 451 AD, and produced the **Chalcedonian Creed** in which is stated that Christ is "truly God and truly man, of a reasonable [rational] soul and body". Doctrinal errors tend to reappear and it is necessary to define the human nature of Christ correctly.

Jesus Christ did not descend from Adam by ordinary generation (cf. Q15). Instead, He was conceived by the power of the Holy Spirit (not "by the Holy Spirit", as in human procreation). The human nature of Jesus Christ, therefore, was derived from Mary but without sin. This teaching guards against the error of the Roman Catholic Church that Jesus Christ's sinlessness is derived from Mary, who remained a virgin throughout her married life. By wrongly equating virginity with sinlessness, Mary is lifted to the higher position of "Mother of God" who must be prayed to in order to influence the Son of God to hear our prayers. The Bible, however, teachers that Mary had other children by Joseph (Matt. 1:25; Mark 6:3). If Mary had remained a virgin throughout her marriage, she would have sinned against her husband and her God (cf. 1 Cor. 7:3-5). The answer also guards against **Modernism**, which rejects the virgin birth and the miracles in the Bible.

Six

THE WORK OF CHRIST IN SALVATION

Q22. What offices does Christ execute as our Redeemer?
A22. Christ as our Redeemer executes the offices of a prophet[1], of a priest[2], and of a king[3], both in His state of humiliation and exaltation.

1 Acts 3:22, For Moses truly said to the fathers, *'The LORD your God will raise up for you a Prophet like me from your brethren. Him you shall hear in all things, whatever He says to you.'*

2 Heb. 5:6, As *He* also *says* in another *place*: "You are a priest forever according to the order of Melchizedek."

3 Psalm 2:6, Yet I have set My King on My holy hill of Zion.

Comments

God indicated that the coming Saviour would occupy the three offices by raising up men in the Old Testament who were prophets, priests, or kings, e.g. Abraham, Moses, and David. None of those men fulfilled the three offices fully or perfectly. Jesus Christ, as the only Mediator between God and man, fulfilled the three offices fully and perfectly.

Man is made up of body and soul in his *person*, and he is made up of mind, heart (or affection) and will in his *personality*. The conscience may be regarded as the effect of the interaction between the three faculties (Rom. 2:14-15). When saved, he is redeemed in his total person by Jesus Christ, and he is transformed in his total personality by the Holy Spirit. Similarly, a church that truly acknowledges Christ's headship submits to Him in His three offices.

Q23. How does Christ execute the office of a prophet?
A23.[1] Christ executes the office of a prophet in revealing[1], by His word[2], and Spirit[3], the will of God for the salvation of His people.

1. John 1:18, No one has seen God at any time. The only begotten Son, who is in the bosom of the Father, He has declared *Him*.

2. John 20:31, But these are written that you may believe that Jesus is the Christ, the Son of God, and that believing you may have life in His name.

3. John 14:26, But the Helper, the Holy Spirit, whom the Father will send in My name, He will teach you all things, and bring to your remembrance all things that I said to you.

Comments

The function of a prophet was to reveal God's will. In 1 Corinthians 3:11, Jesus Christ is revealed as the only foundation upon which the church is built. In Ephesians 2:20, "the apostles and prophets" is a reference to their writings, which constitute the Old and New Testaments, i.e. the whole Bible. Since the Bible reveals Christ and the salvation wrought by Him in His death and resurrection (Luke 24:44-48; 2 Tim. 2:16-17), it may be said that "the apostles and prophets" constitute the foundation of the church, with Christ as the

---

[1] We have changed "revealing to us... the will of God for our salvation" to "revealing ... the will of God for the salvation of His people".

6. THE WORK OF CHRIST IN SALVATION

chief cornerstone. The important role of Scripture in revealing Jesus Christ and the way of salvation, i.e. the gospel, is emphasized.

Just as the Scripture cannot be separated from Jesus Christ, it cannot be separated from the Holy Spirit. The Holy Spirit inspired the writing of the Scripture (2 Tim. 3:16-17; 2 Pet. 1:20-21). The Holy Spirit regenerates sinners (John 3:5-8) by the hearing of God's word (Rom. 10:17; 1 Pet. 1:23). The Holy Spirit causes spiritual growth in the believer by the word of God (1 Pet. 1:22). We are not surprised that the person who is born again will hunger for the word of God (1 Pet. 2:2; Matt. 4:4). The enlightenment of the Holy Spirit is needed for the correct understanding of God's word (John 14:26).

The church that is submitted to Christ as its Head will be submitted to Him as prophet. This means that the revelation of God, or doctrine, will be valued. Practically, the church will make the preaching and teaching of God's word central in its life. It will also adopt a good confession of faith as its doctrinal basis.

Q24. How does Christ execute the office of a priest?
A24.[2] Christ executes the office of a priest, in His once offering up Himself a sacrifice for the sins of His people to satisfy divine justice[1], and to reconcile them to God[2], and in making continual intercession for them[3].

1 Heb. 9:28, So Christ was offered once to bear the sins of many. To those who eagerly wait for Him He will appear a second time, apart from sin, for salvation.

2 Heb. 2:17, Therefore, in all things He had to be made like *His* brethren, that He might be a merciful and faithful High Priest in things *pertaining* to God, to make propitiation for the sins of the people.

3 Heb. 7:25, Therefore He is also able to save to the uttermost those who come to God through Him, since He always lives to make intercession for them.

---

[2]We have added "for the sins of His people" and adjusted the rest of the answer accordingly.

Comments

Aaron was the High Priest in the nation of Israel, and was succeeded by his sons. Jesus Christ's priesthood is "according to the order of Melchizedek", which means that it is superior to that of Aaron. Instead of offering up an animal sacrifice, He offered up Himself as the perfect sacrifice for the sins of His people, thereby reconciling them to God. Christ continues to intercede for His people in heaven, i.e. to speak on their behalf, on the basis of His death for them.

A true believer shows his submission to Christ's priesthood by his life of worship and prayer. There is a love for God's people such that he regularly gathers with them (Acts 2:42; Heb. 10:24-25; 1 John 3:14). Similarly, a church that is submitted to the priesthood of Christ would have biblical worship, instead of pandering to the carnal desire, e.g. dancing, entertaining one another with song presentations, seeking personal enjoyment in hand-clapping and repetitive singing, etc.

Q25. How does Christ execute the office of a king?
A25. Christ executes the office of a king in subduing His people unto Himself[1], in ruling and defending them[2], and in restraining and conquering all His and their enemies[3].

1 Psalm 110:3, *Your people shall be volunteers in the day of Your power; in the beauties of holiness, from the womb of the morning, You have the dew of Your youth.*

2 Matt. 2:6, *But you, Bethlehem, in the land of Judah, are not the least among the rulers of Judah; for out of you shall come a Ruler who will shepherd My people Israel.*

3 1 Cor. 15:25, *For He must reign till He has put all enemies under His feet.*

Comments

The function of a king in the Old Testament was to rule over His people and to lead them into battles. Christ subdues the chosen

6. THE WORK OF CHRIST IN SALVATION

people of God through the preaching of the gospel, in the power of His Spirit. He gives them an inner desire to know His word and the ability to obey it, at the same time defending them from their enemies. The enemies are mainly spiritual ones (1 Pet. 5:8), including temptations from without (1 Cor. 10:13), sin from within (Gal. 5:24-25), and death (1 Cor. 15:26, 54). Christ also restrains the evil that befalls His people (Job 1:12; 2:6), and conquers their enemies by bringing them to nothing, as happened to Herod Agrippa I (Acts 12:21-23), or converting them, as happened to Saul (Acts 9:15). Christ treats the enemies of His people as His personal enemies (cf. Acts 9:4, 5).

A true believer shows his submission to Christ's kingship by obedience to His word (John 14:21; 1 John 2:3-6). In the church, submission to Christ's kingship is shown by having biblical church government, which includes church discipline, and engaging in outreach to win souls to Christ and to plant churches. The three offices of Christ are to be applied to the Christian life, as well as to the church, in that number and that order, viz. prophethood, priesthood, and kingship (cf. Rom. 6:17; 1 Tim. 1:7).

Q26.[3] What constituted Christ's humiliation?
A26. Christ's humiliation included His being born, in a low condition[1], made under the law[2]; undergoing the miseries of this life[3], the wrath of God[4], and the cursed death of the cross[5, 6]; being buried, and continuing under the power of death for a time[7].

1 Luke 2:7, And she brought forth her firstborn Son, and wrapped Him in swaddling cloths, and laid Him in a manger, because there was no room for them in the inn.

2 Gal. 4:4, But when the fullness of the time had come, God sent forth His Son, born of a woman, born under the law.

---

[3]The question has been simplified from, "Wherein did Christ's humiliation consist?" The answer has been tidied up under three sections, separated by semicolons.

3 Isa. 53:3, He is despised and rejected by men, a Man of sorrows and acquainted with grief. And we hid, as it were, *our* faces from Him; He was despised, and we did not esteem Him.

4 Matt. 27:46, And about the ninth hour Jesus cried out with a loud voice, saying, "Eli, Eli, lama sabachthani?" that is, *"My God, My God, why have You forsaken Me?"*

5 Phil. 2:8, And being found in appearance as a man, He humbled Himself and became obedient to *the point of* death, even the death of the cross.

6 Gal. 3:13, Christ has redeemed us from the curse of the law, having become a curse for us (for it is written, *"Cursed is everyone who hangs on a tree"*).

7 Matt. 12:40, For as Jonah was three days and three nights in the belly of the great fish, so will the Son of Man be three days and three nights in the heart of the earth.

Comments

When the Son of God became Man, He veiled His deity and took on frail humanity (Phil. 2:5-8). He did not "empty" (Greek, "kenosis", in Phil. 2:7) Himself of deity, as claimed in the **"kenosis theory"** (cf. Luke1:35; Acts 3:14-15). While we do not have a choice in the circumstances of our birth, Christ chose to be born in a humble setting, into the family of a carpenter, instead of a palace. He willingly placed Himself under the law, fulfilling it perfectly on behalf of His people. This has been called the "active obedience" of Christ which, together with His "passive obedience" of dying on the cross, fully paid for the sins of His people (Gal. 4:4-5; Rom. 4:25) and secured the necessary righteousness for them to be accepted by God (2 Cor. 5:21).

While on earth, Christ was hungry (Matt. 21:18), sad (John 11:35), provoked (John 2:14-17), tempted (Heb. 4:15), and in agony (Luke 22:44). While hanging on the cross, the full force of God's wrath for the sins of His people fell upon Christ (2 Cor. 5:21). His was no ordinary death in that He willingly bore the curse due to the sins of His people (Gal. 3:13). Christ identified Himself with

6. THE WORK OF CHRIST IN SALVATION

His people even in death, by being buried and remaining for a time under its power.

Q27.[4] What constitute Christ's exaltation?
A27. Christ's exaltation includes His rising again from the dead on the third day[1], ascending up into heaven, sitting at the right hand of God the Father[2], and coming to judge the world at the last day[3].

1. 1 Cor. 15:4, And that He was buried, and that He rose again the third day according to the Scriptures.

2. Mark 16:19, So then, after the Lord had spoken to them, He was received up into heaven, and sat down at the right hand of God.

3. Acts 17:31, Because He has appointed a day on which He will judge the world in righteousness by the Man whom He has ordained. He has given assurance of this to all by raising Him from the dead.

Comments

The resurrection of Christ shows that the last stronghold of Satan has been overcome, thereby guaranteeing the resurrection of His people in glory (1 Cor. 15:20-21, 56-57). The resurrection of Christ has been denied by the liberals, when it is a fundamental teaching of the Bible (1 Cor. 15:12-19). Christ rose "on the third day", not "after three days". His ascension was a literal one, seen by the apostles and disciples (Acts 1:9-11). "To sit at the right hand" is a figurative expression, since God has no bodily parts. It means "the place of honour and authority" which Christ now occupies (Matt. 28:18; Acts 5:31; Phil. 2:9-10).

Just as certainly as Christ has died, risen from the dead, and been glorified, He will return to judge the world. No one knows the time of His return (Matt. 24:36). There will be no signs *indicating* His

---
[4]The question and answer have been slightly adjusted to accord with the earlier question.

return, which must not be confused with the signs *accompanying* His return (Matt. 24:29-30; Acts 2:19-20; Rev. 6:12-17). The return of the Lord is compared to the flood of Noah and the thief in the night (Matt. 24:37, 43), showing that no one will know when that happens (Matt. 24:36, 44). What is important for us is that we be ready!

Seven

THE SPIRIT'S WORK IN SALVATION

Q28.[1] How are God's elect made partakers of the redemption purchased by Christ?
A28. God's elect are made partakers of the redemption purchased by Christ, by the effectual application of it to them[1] by His Holy Spirit[2].

1 John 1:12, But as many as received Him, to them He gave the right to become children of God, to those who believe in His name.

2 Titus 3:5-6, Not by works of righteousness which we have done, but according to His mercy He saved us, through the washing of regeneration and renewing of the Holy Spirit, whom He poured out on us abundantly through Jesus Christ our Savior.

Comments

In salvation, all three Persons of the Holy Trinity are involved: the Father chose certain individuals to be saved, the Son came to redeem them from their sins, and the Holy Spirit applies the finished work

---
[1]By replacing "we" with "God's elect" in the question, the answer has been adjusted accordingly.

of Christ to the elect. The doctrine of "Invincible Grace" teaches that the work of the Spirit in saving the elect will always be successful. The word "invincible" means "unconquerable". It is better than the commonly used word "irresistible", since this word easily conveys the wrong idea that man is incapable of resisting the work of the Spirit in his life (cf. Acts 7:51).

The expression "effectual application" means to apply in such a way as to accomplish the intended purpose. Since Christ's death was to redeem the elect, the Holy Spirit applies the finished work of Christ to the elect in such a way that they are truly saved. Truth often becomes error by the process of addition, subtraction, or distortion. The Roman Catholics err by *addition*, teaching that God saves with man's co-operation, by the use of the sacraments of the mass, confession of sins to the priest, baptism, etc. The Modernists err by *subtraction*, teaching that man can be saved by his own power, without the need of the supernatural work of the Holy Spirit. The Arminians err by *distortion*, teaching that the Holy Spirit works in man only if he first repents and believes.

Q29.[2] How does the Spirit apply to God's elect the redemption purchased by Christ?
A29. The Spirit applies to God's elect the redemption purchased by Christ by working repentance and faith in them[1, 2], and by uniting them to Christ in their effectual calling[3].

1 Acts 11:18, When they heard these things they became silent; and they glorified God, saying, "Then God has also granted to the Gentiles repentance to life."

2 Eph. 2:8, For by grace you have been saved through faith, and that not of yourselves; *it is* the gift of God.

3 Phil. 1:29, For to you it has been granted on behalf of Christ, not only to believe in Him, but also to suffer for His sake.

---

[2]Apart from changing "us" to "God's elect" in the question, we have added "repentance" to the answer. This makes the answer correspond to the responsibility of man to repent and believe, as found in Q84, later. The last Bible reference has been changed from Eph. 3:17 to Phil. 1:29.

7. THE SPIRIT'S WORK IN SALVATION

Comments

It is the responsibility of man to repent and believe (more of that in Q84). Man, being "dead in trespasses and sins" (Eph. 2:1), is unable of himself to repent and believe. God has to give him faith and repentance, and unite him to Christ. The Spirit does not save by forcing the person against his will, but by changing his nature so that he willingly comes to Christ despite initial difficulties.

Why are there people who hear the gospel but are not saved? The reason is not in the gospel itself, nor in the preacher himself, nor in the hearer himself. Of course, the gospel must be preached clearly and correctly, the preacher must preach in faith and in the power of the Spirit, and the hearer must not resist the Holy Spirit but respond to the call of the gospel. Ultimately, the Holy Spirit must call the sinner effectually before he can be saved. This is illustrated in the raising of Lazarus to life, for it was by the hearing of Christ's word and by the work of the Spirit that he was raised (John 11:43-44; 1 Thess. 2:13).

Q30. What is effectual calling?
A30.[3] Effectual calling is the work of God's Spirit[1] whereby, enlightening the minds of the elect in the knowledge of God[2, 3], convincing them of their sin and misery[4], and renewing their wills[5], He does persuade and enable them to embrace Jesus Christ freely preached to all in the gospel[6].

1 John 16:8, And when He has come, He will convict the world of sin, and of righteousness, and of judgment.

2 Acts 17:23, For as I was passing through and considering the objects of your worship, I even found an altar with this inscription:

---

[3]The order of "mind, heart, and will" is followed instead of the original answer, and Jesus Christ is "freely preached to all" instead of "freely offered to us". Furthermore, it is not just the knowledge of Christ, but of God, that the original reference, viz. Acts 26:18, speaks of. The first reference, viz. 2 Tim. 1:9, has been replaced by John 16:18, since we are dealing with the work of the Spirit, not that of the Father, in salvation.

TO THE UNKNOWN GOD. Therefore, the One whom you worship without knowing, Him I proclaim to you.

3 Acts 26:18, To open their eyes, *in order* to turn *them* from darkness to light, and *from* the power of Satan to God, that they may receive forgiveness of sins and an inheritance among those who are sanctified by faith in Me.

4 Acts 2:37, Now when they heard *this*, they were cut to the heart, and said to Peter and the rest of the apostles, "Men *and* brethren, what shall we do?"

5 Ezek. 36:26, I will give you a new heart and put a new spirit within you; I will take the heart of stone out of your flesh and give you a heart of flesh.

6 John 6:44-45, No one can come to Me unless the Father who sent Me draws him; and I will raise him up at the last day. It is written in the prophets, 'And they shall all be taught by God.' Therefore everyone who has heard and learned from the Father comes to Me.

Comments

Among those who hear the gospel, only the effectually called are saved. According to the Parable of the Sower (Luke 8:4-15), those who are not saved either: (i) do not respond to the gospel; (ii) respond by having temporary faith; or (iii) respond by having fruitless faith. Only those who respond with a fruitful faith are saved. This comes about by the threefold work of the Spirit: (i) in enlightening their minds so that they know the true God; (ii) in convicting them of their sin against God and of the misery of their lives; and (iii) in renewing their wills so that they can respond to the call of the gospel. By this three-fold work, the Holy Spirit persuades and enables them to trust in Christ alone for salvation.

The gospel may be summarized as the message of "Jesus Christ and Him crucified" (1 Cor. 2:2). Jesus Christ must be shown to be the only Saviour of sinners, and His death must be shown to be the only way by which sinners are to be saved. The gospel must be preached to all alike, for we are not given to know who are elect

7. THE SPIRIT'S WORK IN SALVATION

until they are saved. There are Christians who believe that Jesus Christ being "freely preached to all" is different from "freely offered to all" because the latter implies insincerity on the part of God, who never intended salvation for the non-elect. However, it is not for us to judge God but to offer Christ freely to all as commanded in the Great Commission. In order not to stumble such brethren, we have replace the word "offered" with "preach", believing that the important thing is to preach "freely to all", without discriminating between the hearers.

Eight

THE BENEFITS OF SALVATION IN THIS LIFE

Q31. What benefits do they who are effectually called, partake of in this life?
A31. They who are effectually called, do in this life partake of justification[1], adoption[2], sanctification, and the various benefits which either accompany, or flow from them[3].

1 Rom. 8:30, Moreover whom He predestined, these He also called; whom He called, these He also justified; and whom He justified, these He also glorified.

2 Eph. 1:5, Having predestined us to adoption as sons by Jesus Christ to Himself, according to the good pleasure of His will.

3 1 Cor. 1:30, But of Him you are in Christ Jesus, who became for us wisdom from God—and righteousness and sanctification and redemption.

Comments

The benefits enjoyed by believers in this life may be divided into two categories: (i) those that definitely accompany salvation; and (ii) those that arise from the definite benefits and, therefore, might not be experienced immediately and in full measure. Justification, adoption and sanctification belong to the first category, while those belonging to the second category are given in Q35.

Q32. What is justification?
A32.[1] **Justification is an act of God's free grace whereby those effectually called are pardoned of all their sins**[1,2]**, and accepted as righteous in His sight**[3] **because of the righteousness of Christ imputed to them**[4]**, and received by faith alone**[5,6]**.**

1 Rom. 3:24, Being justified freely by His grace through the redemption that is in Christ Jesus.

2 Eph. 1:7, In Him we have redemption through His blood, the forgiveness of sins, according to the riches of His grace.

3 2 Cor. 5:21, For He made Him who knew no sin *to be* sin for us, that we might become the righteousness of God in Him.

4 Rom. 5:19, For as by one man's disobedience many were made sinners, so also by one Man's obedience many will be made righteous.

5 Gal. 2:16, Knowing that a man is not justified by the works of the law but by faith in Jesus Christ, even we have believed in Christ Jesus, that we might be justified by faith in Christ and not by the works of the law; for by the works of the law no flesh shall be justified.

6 Phil. 3:9, And be found in Him, not having my own righteousness, which *is* from the law, but that which *is* through faith in Christ, the righteousness which is from God by faith.

Comments

Justification is a declaration or pronouncement by God that a particular person is not guilty in His sight and, therefore, not under

---

[1]The expression, "those effectually called" has been added, and the rest of the sentence adjusted accordingly to the form of the answer to the next question.

8. THE BENEFITS OF SALVATION IN THIS LIFE

condemnation. The person is treated as righteous, i.e. not guilty of wrong doing, although he is not perfectly holy in his person. This is due to the perfect righteousness of Christ imputed to him, i.e. counted as his, while the person's sin is imputed to Jesus Christ when He died on the cross (2 Cor. 5:21). *Imputation* is not to be confused with *infusion*. Christ's righteousness is never infused into the believer, i.e. it never seeps into the believer and becomes part of him. Rather, it is counted as, or treated as, his. By the indwelling of the Holy Spirit, the believer will begin to show righteous living, but his personal righteousness is never good enough to contribute to his own salvation. Justification is a once for all act. It is not a process, and it is unrepeatable. It is *received* by faith, and not *produced* by faith.

The Roman Catholic Church teaches that justification is by faith *plus* works of attending mass, confessing sins, baptism, etc. The Reformation of the 16th century recovered the doctrine of "justification by faith alone", which Martin Luther called "the article of a standing or falling church". An old error among Protestants is the idea of "eternal justification" in which is claimed that the elect are justified from eternity, or at least from the moment Christ finished His work on the cross. This contradicts the teaching of the Bible that justification was planned by God from eternity (Ps. 25:6; 103:17), but takes effect at the point the person believes (Col. 1:21-22; Gal. 2:16; Rom. 8:29-30). A wrong teaching called the **New Perspectives on Paul (NPP)** claims that justification is a declaration by God that the person is already among His covenant people, that it is an ongoing process dependent on the righteousness of the person, and that it will be completed on judgement day.

Q33. What is adoption?
A33[2]. Adoption is an act of God's free grace[1], whereby those justified are received into the number, and have a right to all the privileges of the sons of God, by the indwelling of the Holy Spirit[2, 3].

---

[2]The expression, "by the indwelling of the Holy Spirit" has been added to counter the wrong teaching of the Charismatic movement.

1. 1 John 3:1, Behold what manner of love the Father has bestowed on us, that we should be called children of God! Therefore the world does not know us, because it did not know Him.

2. John 1:12, But as many as received Him, to them He gave the right to become children of God, to those who believe in His name.

3. Rom. 8:14-17, For as many as are led by the Spirit of God, these are sons of God. For you did not receive the spirit of bondage again to fear, but you received the Spirit of adoption by whom we cry out, "Abba, Father." The Spirit Himself bears witness with our spirit that we are children of God, and if children, then heirs—heirs of God and joint heirs with Christ, if indeed we suffer with *Him*, that we may also be glorified together.

Comments

Adoption follows justification logically, but not chronologically. In the experience of a believer, he is justified and adopted as soon as he repents and believes. Many today believe in "the universal brotherhood of man", claiming that we are all the children of God and, therefore, brothers and sisters. That is true only from the point of creation (Acts 17:26), but not from the point of salvation. Spiritually speaking, all unbelievers are the children of the devil (John 8:44). We become the children of God only when converted (Eph. 2:12-13).

Our sonship is by adoption, while Christ's sonship is from eternity. Our adoption does not make us divine in any way, while it makes us joint heirs with Christ (Rom. 8:17). Like justification, adoption is a once for all act of God. It is not a process, and is unrepeatable. It comes about by the indwelling of the Holy Spirit, which occurs at the point of conversion (Gal. 3:2). The **Charismatic movement** wrongly uses Acts 19:1-7 to teach the need of receiving the Holy Spirit *after* conversion, shown in tongue-speaking and prophecy.

Q34. What is sanctification?
A34.[3] Sanctification is the work of God's Spirit[1], whereby the

8. THE BENEFITS OF SALVATION IN THIS LIFE

elect are renewed in the whole man after the image of God[2], and are enabled more and more to die to sin, and live to righteousness[3].

1. 2 Thess. 2:13, But we are bound to give thanks to God always for you, brethren beloved by the Lord, because God from the beginning chose you for salvation through sanctification by the Spirit and belief in the truth.

2. Eph. 4:24, And that you put on the new man which was created according to God, in true righteousness and holiness.

3. Rom. 6:11, Likewise you also, reckon yourselves to be dead indeed to sin, but alive to God in Christ Jesus our Lord.

Comments

Unlike justification and adoption, sanctification is not a once for all act of God but it is a process carried out by the Holy Spirit in conjunction with the effort of man. It does not mean that man's work is equal to that of God, but rather that God works in such a way as to involve the work of man (Phil. 2:12-13 cf. Col. 1:29). Two objections often encountered with "justification by faith alone" are cleared up by the correct view of sanctification. The first objection is that the believer may continue to live in sin. However, when a person is truly converted, he is transformed by the Holy Spirit to have holy desires and enabled to live in obedience to God (Rom. 8:12-14; Gal. 5:19-24). The second objection is that the believer needs to show good works together with faith, otherwise his faith is dead. However, Scripture cannot contradict itself (cf. Eph. 2:8-10; Rom. 3:24). The correct understanding is that "we are justified by faith alone, but the faith that justifies is never alone". In other words, true faith will show itself by good works (James 2:17, 24, 26). Good works are the *fruit* of saving faith, and not the *cause* of saving faith.

A wrong view of sanctification, called the "victorious life" or "higher life" view, is that the believer needs to seek a second experience of the Holy Spirit after conversion to lift him up to "entire

---

[3]Following Spurgeon, we have changed "the work of God's free grace" to "the work of God's Spirit". Also, "the elect" replaces "we".

sanctification", in which he sins less and less, or even becomes sinless. This view of sanctification is also called **Perfectionism**. The believer is encouraged to "let go, and let God take over", contradicting the biblical teaching to flee from temptation and to put to death sins (Rom. 7:7-25; 2 Tim. 2:22). This view was linked to the early **Methodist movement** in America and the **Keswick Convention** in Britain. Higher life teachers make the mistake of using Bible passages that deal with justification to teach sanctification.

Q35. What are the benefits which in this life do accompany or flow from justification, adoption, and sanctification?
A35. The benefits which in this life do accompany or flow from justification, adoption, and sanctification, are assurance of God's love, peace of conscience[1], joy in the Holy Spirit[2], increase of grace[3], and perseverance in it to the end[4].

1. Rom. 5:1-2, 5, Therefore, having been justified by faith, we have peace with God through our Lord Jesus Christ, through whom also we have access by faith into this grace in which we stand, and rejoice in hope of the glory of God. Now hope does not disappoint, because the love of God has been poured out in our hearts by the Holy Spirit who was given to us.

2. Rom. 14:17, For the kingdom of God is not eating and drinking, but righteousness and peace and joy in the Holy Spirit.

3. Prov. 4:18, But the path of the just *is* like the shining sun, that shines ever brighter unto the perfect day.

4. 1 Pet. 1:5, Who are kept by the power of God through faith for salvation ready to be revealed in the last time.

Comments

These benefits do not come automatically to the believer, but must be sought by attending to the means of grace, i.e. hearing God's word, being in fellowship with other believers, engaging in corporate prayer, being active in serving God, etc. (2 Tim. 2:22; 2 Pet. 1:10).

8. THE BENEFITS OF SALVATION IN THIS LIFE

Every believer, however, will find them in due time, and to varying degrees (Rom. 8:31-39; 1 Cor. 15:57).

Effort is needed on the part of the believer to attend to the means of grace and to live a holy and righteous life. It is as we work that God is at work in us (Rom. 6:18-19; Phil. 2:12-13; 1 Pet. 1:22-23). God preserves as the Christian perseveres. The true believer will persevere in the faith to the end of his life (Matt. 10:33; 13:23; Luke 14:27). This is called "Perseverance of the Saints".

Nine

THE BENEFITS OF SALVATION AT DEATH

Q36. What benefits do believers receive from Christ at death?
A36.[1] The souls of believers, at their death, are made perfect in holiness[1] and do immediately pass into glory[2-4]; and their bodies, belonging to Christ[5], do rest in their graves[6] until the resurrection[7].

1 Heb. 12:23, To the general assembly and church of the firstborn *who are* registered in heaven, to God the Judge of all, to the spirits of just men made perfect.

2 Phil. 1:23, For I am hard-pressed between the two, having a desire to depart and be with Christ, *which is* far better.

3 2 Cor. 5:8, We are confident, yes, well pleased rather to be absent from the body and to be present with the Lord.

4 Luke 23:43, And Jesus said to him, "Assuredly, I say to you, today you will be with Me in Paradise."

5 1 Cor. 6:14-15, 19-20, And God both raised up the Lord and will also raise us up by His power. Do you not know that your bodies

---

[1]The expression "belonging to Christ" replaces "being still united to Christ", the Bible reference being changed also from 1 Thess. 4:14 to 1 Cor. 6:14-15, 19-20.

are members of Christ? Shall I then take the members of Christ and make *them* members of a harlot? Certainly not! Or do you not know that your body is the temple of the Holy Spirit *who is* in you, whom you have from God, and you are not your own? For you were bought at a price; therefore glorify God in your body and in your spirit, which are God's.

6 Isa. 57:2, He shall enter into peace; they shall rest in their beds, *each one* walking *in* his uprightness.

7 Job 19:26, And after my skin is destroyed, this *I know*, that in my flesh I shall see God.

Comments

We believe that *dichotomy*, i.e. the teaching that the human person is made up of two components, viz. body and soul (or spirit), is the teaching of Scripture (Gen. 2:7; 1 Pet. 1:9; Acts 2:31), although there are others who believe in *trichotomy* (body, soul, and spirit). The Scriptures used in support of trichotomy (e.g. 1 Thess. 5:23; Heb. 4:12) are capable of reasonable explanations according to the context. For example, "spirit" and "soul" may be used together for emphasis, as in 1 Thessalonians 5:23. At death, body and soul are separated (James 2:26). This is the *intermediate state*. The soul of a believer is led to heaven immediately to be with the Lord (Psalm 23:4). The soul is not: (i) left to wander aimlessly on earth; (ii) in "soul sleep" in which it is unconscious; (iii) in purgatory, where it is purified for ultimate admittance to heaven. The body, which is buried, will return to dust (Gen. 3:9; Acts 13:36) until the day of resurrection.

Christians should prefer burial of the body to cremation, although how the body is disposed off will not affect the resurrection. This is because: (i) godly people in the Bible practised burial (e.g. Gen. 23:19; Acts 2:29; James 2:26); (ii) burning is a symbol of God's judgement (e.g. Matt. 3:10-12; 7:19; 13:41-42; Heb. 6:8; Rev. 20:15); (iii) the body has been redeemed by the Lord and should be disposed off lovingly and respectfully (1 Cor. 6:19-20). We do not treat the body as inherently evil (cf. Gnosticism, under Q9). While alive, Christians should take care of the body instead of harming it

9. THE BENEFITS OF SALVATION AT DEATH

by smoking, drinking, gluttony, etc. Although it is possible to go to extremes, those who live a sedentary lifestyle should engage in exercise so that body and soul are offered up to God in sacrificial service (1 Tim. 4:8 cf. Rom. 12:1-2).

Q37.[2] What benefits do believers receive from Christ at the day of judgement?
A37. At the day of judgement, believers being raised up in glory[1], shall be openly acknowledged and acquitted[2], and made perfectly blessed in body and soul in the full enjoyment of God[3] to all eternity[4].

1. 1 Cor. 15:43, It is sown in dishonor, it is raised in glory. It is sown in weakness, it is raised in power.

2. Matt. 10:32, Therefore whoever confesses Me before men, him I will also confess before My Father who is in heaven.

3. 1 John 3:2, Beloved, now we are children of God; and it has not yet been revealed what we shall be, but we know that when He is revealed, we shall be like Him, for we shall see Him as He is.

4. 1 Thess. 4:17, Then we who are alive *and* remain shall be caught up together with them in the clouds to meet the Lord in the air. And thus we shall always be with the Lord.

Comments

On judgement day, the Lord will bring with Him the souls of the redeemed from heaven (1 Thess. 4:14). The souls will be clothed with glorious bodies that are reconstituted from the elements of the original bodies scattered in the earth at death (1 Cor. 15:43, 49). Believers will be judged together with unbelievers (Luke 8:17; 12:2-3; 1 Cor. 4:5). It would appear that the sins of believers will be

---

[2]In the question, "at the day of judgement" replaces "at the resurrection", to conform with Q39. The answer has been adjusted accordingly. Following Spurgeon, we have included "in body and soul", although Spurgeon puts it as "both in soul and body".

made known to all, although they are acquitted because of what Christ has done to save them. "Justice will be done, and seen to be done." Salvation will be seen clearly to be "by grace, through faith, in Christ alone". How carefully believers must live while on earth! Equally, the good done by believers will all come to light, and they will be rewarded accordingly (Matt. 25:20-23; Rev. 22:12).

The righteous will be separated from the wicked (Matt. 25:32). The righteous will be caught up in the air and taken to be with the Lord (1 Thess. 4:17), to dwell on the new earth, which will be in the new heaven (2 Pet. 3:10-13). There will be no marriage in heaven, but our relationships will be lifted to a higher, and growing, level of blessedness (Mark 12:25).

Q38. What shall be done to the wicked at their death?
A38. The souls of the wicked, at their death, are cast into the torments of hell[1], and their bodies lie in their graves until the resurrection and judgement of the great day[2].

1 Luke 16:22-24, So it was that the beggar died, and was carried by the angels to Abraham's bosom. The rich man also died and was buried. And being in torments in Hades, he lifted up his eyes and saw Abraham afar off, and Lazarus in his bosom. Then he cried and said, 'Father Abraham, have mercy on me, and send Lazarus that he may dip the tip of his finger in water and cool my tongue; for I am tormented in this flame.'

2 John 5:28-29, Do not marvel at this; for the hour is coming in which all who are in the graves will hear His voice and come forth—those who have done good, to the resurrection of life, and those who have done evil, to the resurrection of condemnation.

Comments

At death, all traces of the image of God would have been erased from the unbeliever's soul so that whatever blessing, comfort and restraint of God are withdrawn. The unbeliever's full wickedness becomes

9. THE BENEFITS OF SALVATION AT DEATH

obvious as he is cast into the torments of hell. His body turns to dust like that of the believer, awaiting the day of judgement.

Hell is truly a place of torment. The likes of Esau, Jeroboam the son of Nebat, Ahab, Jezebel, and Judas Iscariot would be there, in the full ugliness of their wickedness. Furthermore, the full force of God's wrath upon the wicked will be experienced. Hell is described as "the furnace of fire", where there will be "wailing and gnashing of teeth" (Matt. 13:42).

Q39. What shall be done to the wicked at the day of judgment?
A39.[3] At the day of judgment[1], the wicked being raised up in dishonour[2], shall be openly sentenced and condemned to the unspeakable torments of body and soul in hell[3], with the devil and his angels for all eternity[4].

1 John 5:28-29, Do not marvel at this; for the hour is coming in which all who are in the graves will hear His voice and come forth—those who have done good, to the resurrection of life, and those who have done evil, to the resurrection of condemnation.

2 Dan. 12:2, And many of those who sleep in the dust of the earth shall awake, some to everlasting life, some to shame *and* everlasting contempt.

3 2 Thess. 1:9, These shall be punished with everlasting destruction from the presence of the Lord and from the glory of His power.

4 Matt. 25:41, Then He will also say to those on the left hand, 'Depart from Me, you cursed, into the everlasting fire prepared for the devil and his angels.'

Comments

The wicked will be resurrected, but with an inglorious and dishonourable body. After being sentenced and condemned, he is thrown,

---

[3]The answer in Keach's Catechism has been adjusted to conform with that of Q37.

body and soul, back into hell to share in the torments of the devil and his angels for ever. This is called the "second death", which is worse than the first (Rev. 20:14; 21:8). God would be seen to be just, while the unbeliever would be seen to deserve the condemnation upon him. **Annihilationism**, which teaches that the souls of the wicked will gradually cease to exist (annihilated), contradicts the teaching of the Bible. (See also under Q18.)

The Bible seems to indicate that heaven is a dynamic place in which are blessed activities and growth in love, knowledge, and glory (Rev. 7:15-17; 21:22-22:5). Similarly, we can expect that hell will be a dynamic place in which is continual wickedness and increase in the sufferings and torments. The torments of hell are unspeakable! How we must be reconciled to God quickly! How we must be urgent in soul-winning!

Part II

THE LAW OF GOD

Ten

THE MORAL LAW

Q40. What is the duty which God requires of man?
A40. The duty which God requires of man is obedience to His revealed will[1,2]**.**

1 Eccl. 12:13, Let us hear the conclusion of the whole matter: fear God and keep His commandments, for this is man's all.

2 Micah 6:8, He has shown you, O man, what *is* good; and what does the LORD require of you but to do justly, to love mercy, and to walk humbly with your God?

Comments

As creatures of God, we have a duty to obey His revealed will. God reveals Himself and His will to man in two main ways, viz. through nature and through His written word, the Bible. The first way is called "natural revelation", by which man knows from creation and his conscience that God is great, good, and governs all things. Man's fallen nature causes him to suppress and distort truths such that he worships the gods of his imagination instead of the true God (Rom. 1:18-25).

The second way God reveals His will is called "special revelation". Through the written word, man is brought to a conviction of his sins, and shown the way of salvation in Jesus Christ. Those who are saved, "by grace, through faith, in Christ alone", are enabled by the Holy Spirit to obey God's revealed will, even if imperfectly, while in this life.

Q41. What did God reveal to man for the rule of his obedience?
A41.[1] The rule which God revealed to man for his obedience is the moral law[1], which is summarized in the Ten Commandments[2,3].

1 Rom. 2:14-15, For when Gentiles, who do not have the law, by nature do the things in the law, these, although not having the law, are a law to themselves, who show the work of the law written in their hearts, their conscience also bearing witness, and between themselves *their* thoughts accusing or else excusing *them*.

2 Deut. 10:4, And He wrote on the tablets according to the first writing, the Ten Commandments, which the LORD had spoken to you in the mountain from the midst of the fire in the day of the assembly; and the LORD gave them to me.

3 Matt. 19:17, So He said to him, "Why do you call Me good? No one *is* good but One, *that is*, God. But if you want to enter into life, keep the commandments."

Comments

God has given us the moral law, which is summarized in the Ten Commandments. The moral law was first "written" on the heart of Adam. In other words, he was given a consciousness of what God required of him. That consciousness, although adversely affected by the Fall, continues to operate in the heart of man so that he is left without excuse for sinning against God (Rom. 2:14-15 cf. 1:20).

God gave the Ten Commandments to the nation of Israel so that the Jews became more guilty, compared to the non-Jews, for breaking His law (Rom. 2:21-24). The moral law should not be confused

---

[1]Following Spurgeon, we have appended the answer of the subsequent question to this one.

with the ceremonial law and the civil law. The ceremonial law governed worship in the nation of Israel in the Old Testament time. The civil law governed the life of the nation. The ceremonial law has been fulfilled by the coming of Jesus Christ (Heb. 10:5-10) so that Christians no longer have to keep it. The civil law ceased to be applicable when the nation of Israel was conquered, first by the Babylonians, then by the Romans. Unlike the ceremonial and the civil laws, the moral law is applicable to all man in all ages (Matt. 5:17).

The modern nation of Israel must not be confused with the Old Testament nation, which served God's purpose until the coming of Christ (Matt. 3:9-11; Mark 2:21-22). Modern Israel does not play any special role in God's plan of salvation. Jews will be saved "by grace, through faith, in Christ alone" just like the non-Jews (Rom. 4:16; 11:23, 30-31). All who believe in Christ, both Jews and Gentiles, constitute the true (spiritual) Israel of God (Rom. 2:29; 11:26; Gal. 6:15-16). Together, they are the children of God and the seed of Abraham (Gal. 3:26, 29). Together, they are members of one body, one flock, the middle wall of separation between them having been broken down by the coming of Christ (Eph. 2:14-17; John 10:16).

Q42. What is the sum of the Ten Commandments?
A42. The sum of the Ten Commandments is to love the Lord our God with all our heart, with all our soul, with all our strength, and with all our mind; and our neighbour as ourselves[1].

1 Matt. 22:37-40, Jesus said to him, " *'You shall love the LORD your God with all your heart, with all your soul, and with all your mind.'* This is *the* first and great commandment. And *the* second *is* like it: *'You shall love your neighbor as yourself.'* On these two commandments hang all the Law and the Prophets."

Comments

Being a summary, we must extend the principles taught in each of the Ten Commandments as widely as possible to our thoughts, words and deeds, covering things to do and things to avoid (cf. Matt. 5:21-22; 27-29). The moral law serves to: (i) expose sins (Rom. 3:20); (ii) convict us of guilt (Rom. 3:19); (iii) drive us to seek salvation in Christ (Gal. 3:24); and (iv) guide us in our sanctification (Eph. 5:26-27; 1 John 5:2-3). Together, the first four commandments have been called the First Table of the Law. They teach us true worship, which includes the object, the manner, the attitude, and the day of worship. The last six commandments together have been called the Second Table of the Law. They teach us how we are to serve God, covering the sanctity of lawful authorities, of life, of marriage, of property, of speech, and of the heart. The Roman Catholic Church and the Lutheran Churches combine the second commandment with the first, and divide the tenth commandment into two, in order to have ten commandments still. This does not make sense since we do not need two commands to teach about covetousness, while obscuring *how* we are to worship God.

The law is good, and is a reflection of God's perfect character. The breaking of any point of the law is tantamount to the breaking of the whole, making us liable to eternal damnation (James 2:10). But thanks be to God, there is deliverance from sin through faith in Jesus Christ (Rom. 8:3-4)! The Lord Jesus Christ summarized the Ten Commandments by the two great commandments of loving God with our whole being and loving our neighbour as ourselves. We do not keep the law in order to be saved, but when saved by grace through faith in Christ, we do keep the law.

Two common errors are made with regard to the Ten Commandments. The first error is to think that faith in Christ must be supplemented by the keeping of the law to make our salvation secure or better. This was the view of the Judaizers in the New Testament time (Gal. 4:9-11; 5:6). The Roman Catholic Church teaches a form of this "faith plus" theology, in which faith in Christ must be supplemented by the works of attending mass, confession of sins, baptism, etc. The Churches of Christ (also called **Campbellites**) mostly believe that baptism is necessary to salvation. Another error, called **Antinomianism**, claims that the Ten Commandments belong to the Jews of the Old Testament and are not relevant to Christians. A variation of this error found today, which calls itself **New Covenant Theology**, wrongly identifies the Ten Commandments with the old covenant and claims that Christians do not have to keep the Ten

10. THE MORAL LAW

Commandments since the old covenant has been replaced by the new (Heb. 8:7ff). In particular, the need to keep the Christian Sabbath is denied with the claim that the fourth commandment is "not repeated" in the New Testament, and therefore not binding upon Christians. The Lord, however, teaches that He did not come to destroy the law, but to fulfill it (Matt. 5:17). He warned His disciples against breaking any of the commandments, or teaching others to do so (Matt. 5:19). He showed that the law required His disciples to be perfect (Matt. 5:48).

Eleven

THE WORSHIP OF GOD

Q43.[1] What is the first commandment?
A43. The first commandment is, "You shall have no other gods before Me."[1]

1 Exodus 20:3

Q44. What is required in the first commandment?
A44.[2] The first commandment requires us to know[1] and acknowledge God to be the only true God, and our God[2], and to worship and glorify Him accordingly[3].

1 1 Chron. 28:9, As for you, my son Solomon, know the God of your father, and serve Him with a loyal heart and with a willing mind; for the LORD searches all hearts and understands all the intent of the thoughts. If you seek Him, He will be found by you; but if you forsake Him, He will cast you off forever.

---

[1]Following Spurgeon, we have left out the preface of the Ten Commandments, believing that it is far better for believers to know each of the ten commandments than to be burdened with too many details. We have changed "Which" to "What" in the questions of all ten commandments.

[2]Since the answer to the next question in the original Catechism only repeats this answer in the negative way, we have chosen to leave it out, as Spurgeon did.

2 Deut. 26:17, Today you have proclaimed the LORD to be your God, and that you will walk in His ways and keep His statutes, His commandments, and His judgments, and that you will obey His voice.

3 Matt. 4:10, Then Jesus said to him, "Away with you, Satan! For it is written, 'You shall worship the LORD your God, and Him only you shall serve.'"

Comments

The first commandment is concerned with the *subject* of true worship. We must worship the true God alone. All other gods are from the imagination of man, instigated by the devil and his agents (1 Cor. 8:5-6; 10:19-20). **Syncretism** is the attempt to combine the worship of various gods. The pagans often find no difficulty worshipping many gods, including that of other religions. There are professing Christians who would gather with others for inter-faith worship, where each prays to his own god, or all engage in âĂIJnon-sectarian prayersâĂİ in which God is addressed in general. Such professing Christians are breaking this commandment.

Just as we reject the many gods of paganism, we also reject the one god of other religions different from the trinitarian God of the Bible. The Jews have an inadequate understanding of the true God, who is trinitarian, and do not know Him personally, i.e. in a saving manner, because salvation is found in Christ alone (John 14:6; 1 Tim. 2:5; 1 John 2:23). The one god of the Jehovah's Witnesses, and of Islam, are not the God of the Bible. Attempting to worship the true God, even if unknown, is different from worshipping one, or many, gods that are not of the Bible (Acts 17:22-23 cf. 1 Cor. 8:5-6; 2 Cor. 11:4). Those attempting to worship the true God are ignorant. They may know the true God only through faith in Jesus Christ (John 14:6). Those worshipping a false god, or gods, will need to abandon them when they come to believe in the true God (Acts 19:19; 1 Thess. 1:9). We believe in religious liberty, tolerance, and courtesy towards others, but that does not mean we have to compromise the principles of our faith. At stake are our faithfulness to God and the salvation of souls. Believing in the wrong god or following the wrong way of salvation will end in eternal damnation.

11. THE WORSHIP OF GOD

Q45.[3] What is the second commandment?
A45. The second commandment is, "You shall not make for yourself a carved image – any likeness of anything that is in heaven above, or that is in the earth beneath, or that is in the water under the earth; you shall not bow down to them nor serve them."[1]

1 Exodus 20:4-5

Q46. What is required in the second commandment?
A46.[4] The second commandment requires the keeping pure[1, 2] all such religious worship and ordinances as God has appointed in His word[3, 4], while forbidding the worshipping of God by images[5], or any other way not appointed in His word[6].

1. Exodus 20:5-6, For I, the LORD your God, *am* a jealous God, visiting the iniquity of the fathers upon the children to the third and fourth *generations* of those who hate Me, but showing mercy to thousands, to those who love Me and keep My commandments.

2. Deut. 32:46, And he said to them: "Set your hearts on all the words which I testify among you today, which you shall command your children to be careful to observe—all the words of this law."

3. Matt. 28:20, "Teaching them to observe all things that I have commanded you; and lo, I am with you always, *even* to the end of the age." Amen.

4. Deut. 12:32, Whatever I command you, be careful to observe it; you shall not add to it nor take away from it.

---

[3] For simplicity, the reason for the commandment (Exodus 20:5-6) has been left out.

[4] We have combined the answers of this and of the subsequent question of the original Catechism, and simplified the answer in the first part to "the keeping pure" instead of "the receiving, observing, and keeping pure and entire". It is sufficient to say "the keeping pure" for that covers "the receiving, observing", while "the keeping entire" is covered by "all such religious worship and ordinances ..."

5 Deut. 4:15-16, Take careful heed to yourselves, for you saw no form when the LORD spoke to you at Horeb out of the midst of the fire, lest you act corruptly and make for yourselves a carved image in the form of any figure: the likeness of male or female.

6 Col. 2:18, Let no one cheat you of your reward, taking delight in *false* humility and worship of angels, intruding into those things which he has not seen, vainly puffed up by his fleshly mind.

Comments

This commandment is concerned with the *manner* of worshipping God. Just as a king is to be approached according to palace protocol, so also God must be worshipped in the way He commanded. In Reformed theology, this is called the Regulative Principle of worship. The non-Reformed principle, which may be called the Permissive Principle (called the Normative Principle in the past) of worship, states that whatever is not forbidden by the Bible is permissible to be practised. This has led to the introduction of images, rosaries, crucifixes, and the burning of incense in the Roman Catholic Church, and to dancing, burning of candles, clapping, and hand waving in many churches today.

Aaron attempted to identify the gold calf with the one, true, God and worshipped it in a pagan way, but the whole exercise was severely rejected as idolatry (Exodus 32:5-10). We would not represent the Lord Jesus Christ in pictures when teaching children the Bible, or with statues and crucifixes in the church building (see Q5). We would not worship the true God in pagan ways, in which are dancing, hand clapping, percussion instruments that produce beats and rhythms rather than melody, and emphasis on human entertainment rather than reverence to God. Instead, the worship of God should include the reading of Scripture, preaching and teaching the word of God, prayer, singing appropriate songs of worship, making the offering, and the breaking of bread (Acts 2:42; 1 Tim. 4:13; Eph. 5:19; 1 Cor. 11:23-24; 16:2). Worship should be God-centred, reverential, and joyful – reflective of the worship in heaven (Rev. 5:8-14).

11. THE WORSHIP OF GOD

Q47. What is the third commandment?
A47. The third commandment is, "You shall not take the name of the LORD your God in vain, for the LORD will not hold him guiltless who takes His name in vain."[1]

1 Exodus 20:7

Q48.[5] What is required in the third commandment?
A48. The third commandment requires the holy and reverent use of God's names[1], titles, attributes[2], ordinances[3], word[4], and works[5].

1. Psalm 29:2, Give unto the LORD the glory due to His name; worship the LORD in the beauty of holiness.

2. Rev. 15:3-4, They sing the song of Moses, the servant of God, and the song of the Lamb, saying: "Great and marvelous *are* Your works, Lord God Almighty! Just and true are Your ways, O King of the saints! Who shall not fear You, O Lord, and glorify Your name? For *You* alone *are* holy. For all nations shall come and worship before You, For Your judgments have been manifested."

3. Eccl. 5:1, Walk prudently when you go to the house of God; and draw near to hear rather than to give the sacrifice of fools, for they do not know that they do evil.

4. Psalm 138:2, I will worship toward Your holy temple, and praise Your name for Your lovingkindness and Your truth; for You have magnified Your word above all Your name.

5. Psalm 105:1-5, Oh, give thanks to the LORD! Call upon His name; make known His deeds among the peoples! Sing to Him, sing psalms to Him; talk of all His wondrous works! Glory in His holy

---

[5] We have left out the next two questions of the original Catechism, as Spurgeon did, since the present answer is adequate. The next two questions are, "What is forbidden in the third commandment?" and "What is the reason annexed to the third commandment?"

name; let the hearts of those rejoice who seek the LORD! Seek the LORD and His strength; seek His face evermore! Remember His marvelous works which He has done, His wonders, and the judgments of His mouth.

Comments

This commandment concerns the *attitude* of worship. Formal worship primarily is referred to, but the way we live should be regarded as worship as well (Rom. 12:1-2). To "take the name of the Lord" is to be identified with Him by faith. It is like when a woman is married, she takes the family name of the husband. Believers should not dishonour God through careless or irreverent use of anything related to Him. Examples are: (i) making loose exclamations like, "My God!" or "Jesus!"; (ii) cracking jokes relating to the Bible; (iii) being lax or inattentive in church meetings; (iv) setting a bad example at the place of work as a Christian.

Based on Matthew 5:33-37, some Christians have wrongly concluded that we should not swear at all. The context, however, shows that the Lord was against indiscriminate swearing. The making of vows and oaths are permitted in weighty matters, e.g. in marriage (cf. Deut. 6:13; Ps. 15:4).

Q49.[6] **What is the fourth commandment?**
A49. **The fourth commandment is, "Remember the Sabbath day, to keep it holy. Six days you shall labor and do all your work, but the seventh day is the Sabbath of the LORD your God. In it you shall do no work: you, nor your son, nor your daughter, nor your male servant, nor your female servant, nor your cattle, nor your stranger who is within your gates."**[1]

1 Exodus 20: 8-11

---

[6]Again, for simplicity, the reason for the commandment (Exodus 20:11) has been left out.

11. THE WORSHIP OF GOD

Q50. What is required in the fourth commandment?
A50.[7] The fourth commandment requires the keeping holy to God such set times as He has appointed in His word, expressly one whole day in seven to be a holy Sabbath to Himself[1-3], the first day of the week being the Christian Sabbath since the resurrection of Christ[4, 5].

1 Exodus 20:11, For *in* six days the LORD made the heavens and the earth, the sea, and all that *is* in them, and rested the seventh day. Therefore the LORD blessed the Sabbath day and hallowed it.

2 Lev. 19:30, You shall keep My Sabbaths and reverence My sanctuary: I *am* the LORD.

3 Deut. 5:12, Observe the Sabbath day, to keep it holy, as the LORD your God commanded you.

4 1 Cor. 16:1-2, Now concerning the collection for the saints, as I have given orders to the churches of Galatia, so you must do also: On the first *day* of the week let each one of you lay something aside, storing up as he may prosper, that there be no collections when I come.

5 Acts 20:7, Now on the first *day* of the week, when the disciples came together to break bread, Paul, ready to depart the next day, spoke to them and continued his message until midnight.

Q51. How is the Sabbath to be sanctified?
A51.[8] The Sabbath is to be sanctified by a holy resting all that day, even from such worldly employments and recreations as are lawful on other days[1], and spending the whole time in the public and private exercises of God's worship[2, 3], except so much as is taken up in the works of necessity, piety, and mercy[4].

---

[7]The last part of the answer is from the answer to the subsequent question of the original Catechism.

[8]We have included the works of piety in the last part of the answer, which is assumed in the original Catechism.

1 Lev. 23:3, Six days shall work be done, but the seventh day *is* a Sabbath of solemn rest, a holy convocation. You shall do no work *on it*; it *is* the Sabbath of the LORD in all your dwellings.

2 Psalm 92:1-2, *It is* good to give thanks to the LORD and to sing praises to Your name, O Most High; to declare Your lovingkindness in the morning, and Your faithfulness every night.

3 Isa. 58:13-14, If you turn away your foot from the Sabbath, *from* doing your pleasure on My holy day, and call the Sabbath a delight, the holy *day* of the LORD honorable, and shall honor Him, not doing your own ways, nor finding your own pleasure, nor speaking *your own* words, then you shall delight yourself in the LORD; and I will cause you to ride on the high hills of the earth, and feed you with the heritage of Jacob your father. The mouth of the LORD has spoken.

4 Matt. 12:3-5, 11-12, But He said to them, "Have you not read what David did when he was hungry, he and those who were with him: how he entered the house of God and ate the showbread which was not lawful for him to eat, nor for those who were with him, but only for the priests? Or have you not read in the law that on the Sabbath the priests in the temple profane the Sabbath, and are blameless?" Then He said to them, "What man is there among you who has one sheep, and if it falls into a pit on the Sabbath, will not lay hold of it and lift *it* out? Of how much more value then is a man than a sheep? Therefore it is lawful to do good on the Sabbath."

Comments

This command concerns the *day* of worship. Given a choice, the first day of the week should be kept as the Christian Sabbath (1 Cor. 16:1-2; Acts 20:7; Rev. 1:10). Some situations do not permit the keeping of Sunday as the Christian Sabbath, e.g. in Muslim states, in which case another day should be used. Some people wrongly refer to passages like Acts 13:5, 14; 17:2 in support of a Saturday Sabbath, when those passages only show that Paul took advantage of the Jewish Sabbath to evangelize the gathered people. Merely attending a worship service on Sunday is not keeping the *day* holy. The weekly Bible Study arranged by the church fall under the category of "such set times as He has appointed in His word" (Heb. 10:24), and should be attended to diligently as well.

Rest does not mean inactivity, but the stopping of one set of activities to do another. It is the example set by God for His people (Heb. 4:10), for their good, and as a witness to the unbelieving world. Practically, work and recreation that are normally done on other days are stopped, e.g. reading the newspapers, watching television, shopping, eating out, washing the car, etc. Instead, time is spent in corporate worship, corporate prayer, evangelism, the Lord's Supper, Bible classes, fellowship, etc.. (cf Acts 2:42, 46-47). When kept with the right spirit, the Lord's day and "such set times" will be blessed to the soul, to the extension of God's kingdom, and to the honour of His name.

Twelve

THE PRESERVATION OF THE FAMILY

Q52. What is the fifth commandment?
A52. The fifth commandment is, "Honor your father and your mother, that your days may be long upon the land which the LORD your God is giving you."[1]

1 Exodus 20:12.

Q53.[1] What is required in the fifth commandment?
A53. The fifth commandment requires the preserving the honour, and performing the duties, belonging to every one in their various positions and relationships as superiors[1-3], inferiors[4], or equals[5].

1 Eph. 5:21-22, Submitting to one another in the fear of God. Wives, submit to your own husbands, as to the Lord.

2 Eph. 6:1, 5, Children, obey your parents in the Lord, for this is right. Bondservants, be obedient to those who are your masters

---

[1]We have left out the next question of the original Catechism which is, "What is the reason annexed to the fifth commandment?"

according to the flesh, with fear and trembling, in sincerity of heart, as to Christ.

3 Rom. 13:1, Let every soul be subject to the governing authorities. For there is no authority except from God, and the authorities that exist are appointed by God.

4 Eph. 6:9, And you, masters, do the same things to them, giving up threatening, knowing that your own Master also is in heaven, and there is no partiality with Him.

5 Rom. 12:10, *Be* kindly affectionate to one another with brotherly love, in honor giving preference to one another.

Comments

The fifth, sixth and seventh commandments may be considered as those that guard the institution of the family, which is the basic unit of the church and the state. The fifth commandment is concerned with *the sanctity of lawful authorities*. It is our duty to respect and obey all legitimate authorities, since they are God-given. In the family, parents have authority over the children, and the husband is the head of the family. In the church, elders are appointed to rule over God's people for their good. In the state, there may be a king/queen or government of some kind. The Bible has much to say about the believing family and the church, while giving sufficient principles to guide believers in their behaviour in the world. No particular form of state government is favoured except that which conforms closely to the principles revealed in the Bible, e.g. justice, mercy, fairness, rewarding the good, punishing wrong, maintaining peace, promoting well-being, etc.

Parents have to teach children obedience to lawful authorities, in an atmosphere of love, and allowing for growth and development in them. Sternness and excessive control cause frustration in the children, provoking them to anger and discouraging them (Col. 3:20). Failure to exercise proper discipline results in self-will and rebellion that manifest in later life – in the family and society. There are those whom we respect as our superiors, others as our inferiors, and yet others as our equals – depending on the position and relationship between us and these people. This is reflected in our attitude, speech,

12. THE PRESERVATION OF THE FAMILY

and actions. How good it is if the respect is accompanied with love instead of terror!

Long life and prosperity are promised to God's people corporately, although this truth applies generally to the individual as well (Eph. 6:2-3). When God's people are careless or indifferent to what is taught in this command, the three institutions of family, church and society become weakened so that anarchy and violence might prevail. The blessing of peace and opportunity to serve God would be removed and lives may be lost (cf. 1 Tim. 2:1-4). Christians have to resist the abuse of authority – whether in the family, church, or state. Resistance is legitimate when the authority is transgressing the biblical limits, and whenever there is direct contradiction against the Bible's teaching (Acts 5:29).

Q54. What is the sixth commandment?
A54. The sixth commandment is, "You shall not murder."[1]

1 Exodus 20:13.

Q55.[2] What is required in the sixth commandment?
A55. The sixth commandment requires all lawful endeavours to preserve our own life and the life of others[1], while forbidding whatever that tends towards taking away human life unjustly[2, 3].

1 Acts 16:28, But Paul called with a loud voice, saying, "Do yourself no harm, for we are all here."

2 Gen. 9:6, Whoever sheds man's blood, by man his blood shall be shed; for in the image of God He made man.

---

[2]Spurgeon kept the negative questions for the sixth, seventh, eight and tenth commandments. We shall keep all the positive questions to all the commandments, and combine the positive and negative answers wherever necessary. We have added "human" to the answer of this question.

85

3 Prov. 24:11-12, Deliver *those who* are drawn toward death, and hold back *those* stumbling to the slaughter. If you say, "Surely we did not know this," does not He who weighs the hearts consider *it*? He who keeps your soul, does He *not* know *it*? And will He *not* render to *each* man according to his deeds?

Comments

This commandment is concerned with *the sanctity of life*. Our lives come from God, through our parents. Since man is made in God's image, life is sacred (Gen. 1:27; 9:6). An animal has life, but it is not created like man (Gen. 1:25). The unjust killing of a human being is murder. The killing of another person may not be tantamount to murder, as when we kill a robber who attempts to take our lives. A Christian who serves in the army may be required to kill in defence of the country, or in a just cause. In this situation, the Christian is not acting in his private capacity, but as a proper agent of the government. Capital punishment, i.e. the killing of those who commit murder, is the prerogative of the government, not of the individual (Gen. 9:6; Rom. 13:4 cf. Matt. 26:52; Acts 25:11).

Suicide is a breaking of this commandment (cf. Job 1:21). Deliberately placing ourselves or others in danger of life is also breaking this commandment, e.g. engaging in life-threatening sports, engaging in dare-devil stunts, etc. Failure to remove a potentially life-threatening situation is also breaking this commandment, e.g. children playing with knives. It is required that we seek our neighbour's good, e.g. warning him of dangers. The highest good we can do to others is to warn them of judgement day and to proclaim the gospel to them (Matt. 16:26; James 5:20).

Q56. What is the seventh commandment?
A56. The seventh commandment is, "You shall not commit adultery."[1]

1 Exodus 20:14.

12. THE PRESERVATION OF THE FAMILY

Q57. What is required in the seventh commandment?
A57. The seventh commandment requires the preservation of chaste thoughts[1, 2], words[3], and actions[4] in ourselves and others.

1 Matt. 5:28, But I say to you that whoever looks at a woman to lust for her has already committed adultery with her in his heart.

2 2 Tim. 2:22, Flee also youthful lusts; but pursue righteousness, faith, love, peace with those who call on the Lord out of a pure heart.

3 Col. 4:6, *Let* your speech always *be* with grace, seasoned with salt, that you may know how you ought to answer each one.

4 Eph. 5:3-4, But fornication and all uncleanness or covetousness, let it not even be named among you, as is fitting for saints; neither filthiness, nor foolish talking, nor coarse jesting, which are not fitting, but rather giving of thanks.

Comments

This commandment is concerned with *the sanctity of marriage*. Sexual desire was included in the creation of Adam and Eve (Gen. 2:24-25) and, therefore, to be regarded as "very good" (Gen. 1:31). It is this need which draws people together in marriage. The Bible condemns the unlawful satisfaction of the sexual urge outside the institution of marriage, which is fornication. Fornication covers illicit sex of all kinds, including rape (Deut. 22:28-29), premarital sex, adultery (Deut. 22:22), homosexuality (Lev. 18:22), and bestiality (sex with animals, Lev. 18:23; 20:15-16).

It is only by the grace of God that we are able to escape such sins (Eph. 2:1; 2 Pet. 1:4). God has graciously provided ways for us to handle the sexual urge: (i) by the gift of continency (i.e. self-control, Matt. 19:12); (ii) by marriage (1 Cor. 7:9); and (iii) by giving us holy desires and opportunities of spiritual pursuits (2 Tim. 2:22). Christians may marry "only in the Lord" (1 Cor. 7:39; 2 Cor. 6:14). If a person becomes a Christian after marriage, he has a duty to keep that marriage as long as the unbelieving partner is willing to remain in it. The Christian is free to divorce and remarry another only if: (i) the spouse commits adultery and is unrepentant; (ii) if there is breaking of the marriage covenant, such as by physical abuse or desertion that cannot be remedied (1 Cor. 7:10-12; Matt. 19:8). Marriage to relatives who are closely related, by *consanguinity* (i.e. by marriage ties) or *affinity* (i.e. by blood ties) is also forbidden (Lev. 18, 20; Matt. 14:4; Mark 6:18; 1 Cor. 5:1). We must guard our hearts against sinning inwardly and by actions (Matt. 5:28; 2 Tim. 2:22).

Thirteen

THE PRESERVATION OF SOCIETY

Q58. What is the eighth commandment?
A58. The eighth commandment is, "You shall not steal."[1]

1 Exodus 20:15.

Q59. What is required in the eighth commandment?
A59.[1] The eighth commandment requires lawful endeavours to further the wealth and well-being of ourselves and others[1,2], while forbidding whatever that tends towards taking away the wealth or well-being of ourselves or others unjustly[3,4].

1. 1 Tim. 5:8, But if anyone does not provide for his own, and especially for those of his household, he has denied the faith and is worse than an unbeliever.

2. Prov. 28:19, He who tills his land will have plenty of bread, but he who follows frivolity will have poverty enough!

---

[1]We have couched the last part of the answer according to that of the sixth commandment, leaving out "all" in "all lawful endeavours" since we are here dealing with property, not life. The emphasis is on the lawfulness of the endeavours and not on the endeavours *per se*. Also, "well-being" replaces "outward state".

3 Eph. 4:28, Let him who stole steal no longer, but rather let him labor, working with *his* hands what is good, that he may have something to give him who has need.

4 Prov. 21:17, He who loves pleasure *will be* a poor man; he who loves wine and oil will not be rich.

Comments

The eighth, ninth and tenth commandments may be considered as those that guard the interactions between man and man, so that society may be preserved and not descend into chaos. The eighth commandment is concerned with *the sanctity of private property*. The right to private property is ordained by God (Gen. 1:29; Acts 5:4), who is the ultimate owner of all things (Psalm 50:10-11). God has given different abilities and opportunities to men to gain wealth and to improve their lot (Prov. 6:6-8; Matt. 25:19-46). One's wealth may have been given, as a gift or an inheritance (Num. 36:7-9; 2 Cor. 12:14; Eph. 4:28; Phil. 4:18), or it may have been earned (Prov. 27:23, 27; Eph. 4:28; 2 Thess. 3:10; 1 Tim. 5:8). Stealing is unjustly taking away what belongs to others. This may happen secretly or openly, obviously or subtly. A burglar may secretly, but obviously, take away what is yours. A bad government may openly and subtly take away the hard-earned wealth of some to give to others in the name of "the equal distribution of wealth". Being lazy and sleeping on the job is stealing the employer's time and getting paid for inadequate work done. Being wasteful at a job costs the employer money and is a form of stealing from him.

Christians may work hard, and use their ingenuity, to gain wealth honestly and justly. Money is needed to support those dependent on us, e.g. our children and aged parents (2 Cor. 12:14; 1 Tim. 5:8, 16). Money is needed to support gospel work (1 Cor. 16:1-2; Phil. 4:18; 1 Tim 5:17). It is legitimate to live comfortably – within our means, and within reason. The danger lies in "the love for money", which is a root of all kinds of evil (1 Tim. 6:10). Being rich is not a sin, although riches can become a snare (Matt. 19:24). A poor person may be guilty of greed, while a rich person may be truly godly (1 Tim. 6:17-19).

13. THE PRESERVATION OF SOCIETY

Q60. What is the ninth commandment?
A60. The ninth commandment is, "You shall not bear false witness against your neighbour."[1]

1 Exodus 20:16.

Q61. What is required in the ninth commandment?
A61. The ninth commandment requires the maintaining and promoting of truth between man and man[1], and of our own[2, 3], and our neighbour's good name[4], especially in witness-bearing[5], while forbidding whatever is prejudicial to truth, or injurious to our own or our neighbour's good name[6, 7].

1. Zech. 8:16, These *are* the things you shall do: speak each man the truth to his neighbor; give judgment in your gates for truth, justice, and peace.

2. 1 Pet. 3:16, Having a good conscience, that when they defame you as evildoers, those who revile your good conduct in Christ may be ashamed.

3. Acts 25:10, So Paul said, "I stand at Caesar's judgment seat, where I ought to be judged. To the Jews I have done no wrong, as you very well know."

4. 3 John 12, Demetrius has a *good* testimony from all, and from the truth itself. And we also bear witness, and you know that our testimony is true.

5. Prov. 14:5, 25, A faithful witness does not lie, but a false witness will utter lies. A true witness delivers souls, but a deceitful *witness* speaks lies.

6. Eph. 4:25, Therefore, putting away lying, *"Let each one of you speak truth with his neighbor,"* for we are members of one another.

7. Psalm 15:3, He *who* does not backbite with his tongue, nor does evil to his neighbor, nor does he take up a reproach against his friend.

Comments

This commandment is concerned with *the sanctity of speech*. Two basic matters are involved: speaking the truth, and keeping a good name. Putting it another way, we must refrain from lying and slander. God is called "LORD God of truth" (Psalm 31:5). Jesus Christ is "the way, the truth, and the life" (John 14:6). Satan is the father of lies (John 8:44). All those who are saved, through faith in Christ, come to know God, and the truth. It is our duty to be perfect even as our Father in heaven is perfect (Matt. 5:48). When we fail to tell the truth, we harm our own name, and possibly the name of others, especially when called upon to be a witness. It is essential that, in everyday life, Christians "speak the truth in love", with the view of edifying others (Eph. 4:15, 25). In witness-bearing, the rule is to "speak the truth, the whole truth, and nothing but the truth" (Prov. 12:22). Sanctified speech also includes abstaining from gossip (1 Tim. 5:13), boasting (James 3:5) and uttering unwholesome words (Eph. 4:29, 31; 1 Pet. 2:1). There are times when we must speak up for the truth and not commit the "sin of silence" (Ezek. 3:18; Esther 4:14).

Excuses are often used to cover up the breaking of this commandment, under the guise of "white lies" and "lies of necessity". "White lies" are supposedly harmless, told to avoid hurting others, or to flatter them. But this is contrary to biblical teaching (Eph. 4:25; 1 John 2:21). "Lies of necessity" are supposedly unavoidable in certain circumstances. It is claimed that Abraham lied to save his life (Gen. 12:13, 19; 20:2, 5, 12), and the midwives lied to Pharaoh to save lives (Ex. 1:19-21). However, two points must be noted: (i) there is no indication in Scripture that God approved of Abraham's lie; (ii) the rules of war are different from the rules of peace, which applied to the situation faced by the midwives. Camouflage, deception, and outwitting the enemies are legitimate and accepted strategies of warfare. Another point to note is that withholding information from those who have no right, or need, to know is different from telling outright lies. For example, you need not reveal to a robber that your husband is away, or where your jewellery is kept.

13. THE PRESERVATION OF SOCIETY

Q62. What is the tenth commandment?
A62. The tenth commandment is, "You shall not covet your neighbor's house; you shall not covet your neighbour's wife, nor his male or female servant, nor his ox, nor his donkey, nor anything that is your neighbour's."[1]

1 Exodus 20:17.

Q63. What is required in the tenth commandment?
A63.[2] The tenth commandment requires full contentment with our own condition[1,2], with a right and charitable frame of spirit towards our neighbour, and all that is his[3,4], while forbidding all unworthy emotions and desires toward anything that belongs to him[5].

1 Heb. 13:5, *Let your* conduct *be* without covetousness; *be* content with such things as you have. For He Himself has said, *"I will never leave you nor forsake you."*

2 1 Tim. 6:6, Now godliness with contentment is great gain.

3 Gal. 5:26, Let us not become conceited, provoking one another, envying one another.

4 James 3:14, 16, But if you have bitter envy and self-seeking in your hearts, do not boast and lie against the truth. For where envy and self-seeking *exist*, confusion and every evil thing *are* there.

5 Col. 3:5, Therefore put to death your members which are on the earth: fornication, uncleanness, passion, evil desire, and covetousness, which is idolatry.

---

[2]In the last part of this answer, we have used a considerably shortened version of the answer of the next question in the original Catechism.

Comments

This commandment is concerned with *the sanctity of the heart*. Unlike all the other commandments, this one speaks only of the inward state of the heart. Out of the heart flows all kinds of evil (Mark 7: 20-23). The believer must guard against any stirring of discontent with his own situation, which will lead to envy, then covetousness, and finally entanglement in sinful desires, if not committing physical acts of sin (James 1:14-15; 3:14-16). Covetousness is idolatry (Eph. 5:5 cf. Matt. 5:21-22; 27-28). Paul, who was perfect with regard to external righteousness (Phil. 3:6), was convicted of his inner corruption by this law (Rom. 7:7). The believer has no choice, but to be perfect (i.e. to strive for perfection), as the Father in heaven is perfect (Matt. 5:48).

God gives different abilities and opportunities to all, to be used to the utmost for His glory (1 Cor. 3:11-13; 10:31; 12:4-7). He does not demand from His children more than they are able to give (Matt. 25:14ff). We are to have a charitable frame of spirit toward those who are more able, and have done better, than us. The key to guarding the heart is to find full contentment in God (Gen. 15:1; Phil. 4:11-12). This will guard us not only from discontent, but also from the opposite sins of fatalism and sloth (Matt. 25:29).

Fourteen

THE PENALTY OF THE LAW

Q64. Is any man able perfectly to keep the commandments of God?
A64.[1] No mere man, since the Fall, is able in his life perfectly to keep the commandments of God[1], but does daily break them in thought[2], word[3], and deed[4].

1 Eccl. 7:20, For *there is* not a just man on earth who does good and does not sin.

2 Gen. 8:21, And the LORD smelled a soothing aroma. Then the LORD said in His heart, "I will never again curse the ground for man's sake, although the imagination of man's heart *is* evil from his youth; nor will I again destroy every living thing as I have done."

3 James 3:2, 8, For we all stumble in many things. If anyone does not stumble in word, he *is* a perfect man, able also to bridle the whole body. ... But no man can tame the tongue. *It is* an unruly evil, full of deadly poison.

4 Rom. 3:23, For all have sinned and fall short of the glory of God.

---

[1]Following Spurgeon, we have replaced "his" with "this" in the answer.

Comments

Apart from Jesus Christ, no one has kept God's law perfectly since the Fall. Fallen man has a sinful nature, inherited from Adam and Eve, which makes him unacceptable in heaven. Fallen man also breaks God's law daily in thought, word, and deed, making him guilty before God. The law of God performs the functions of: (i) revealing the holiness of God (Rom. 7:12); (ii) exposing the sinfulness of man (Rom. 7:7); (iii) driving sinful man to Jesus Christ for salvation (Gal. 3:24-25); and (iv) setting the standard of holiness for Christians to live by (Matt. 6:17-20).

There are two common errors that Christians must beware of. The first error is **Perfectionism**, which claims that it is possible for Christians to achieve, in this life, a level of holiness in which he no longer sins. Those who believe this often use slogans like "victorious Christian living", "the secret of higher life", and "let go, and let God". It is claimed that those who have "learned the secret" are able to live a kind of sinless perfection. This, however, is contrary to the teaching of the Bible (Eccl. 7:20; 1 John 1:8, 10). (See also on Q34.) The Roman Catholic Church teaches that some Christians live so well that they are regarded as "saints", who have accumulated more merits than are required by God, so that others may draw from them some merits to make up for their own imperfection.

Another error is **Antinomianism**, which means to be against the law ("anti" and "nomos"). It is claimed that since Christ has satisfied the law for us, there is no obligation for us to keep God's commandments. Some antinomians hold a "two-man" theory of the human personality. It is claimed that when a Christian sins, it is the "old man" in him who is to blame. The Bible, however, teaches that the Christian is a "new creation" in Christ (2 Cor. 5:17), and that he has put off the old man and his deeds (Col. 3:9). A Christian will strive to be perfect, attempting to keep the law (Matt. 5:17-21, 48). Although he is troubled by remaining sins, he thanks God for forgiveness in Christ, and strives to live a holy life by the power of the Holy Spirit (Rom. 7:24-8:1).

14. THE PENALTY OF THE LAW

Q65. Are all transgressions of the law equally heinous?
A65. Some sins in themselves, and by reason of various aggravations, are more heinous in the sight of God than others[1, 2].

1 John 19:11, Jesus answered, "You could have no power at all against Me unless it had been given you from above. Therefore the one who delivered Me to you has the greater sin."

2 1 John 5:16, If anyone sees his brother sinning a sin *which does not lead* to death, he will ask, and He will give him life for those who commit sin not *leading* to death. There is sin *leading* to death. I do not say that he should pray about that.

Comments

It is worse to sin against God than to sin against man. It is worse to sin deliberately than to sin ignorantly. Those who have more knowledge and opportunities are held more responsible than those who have less. This applies to Christians and non-Christians alike (Ezek. 8:6, 13, 15; Luke 12:47-48). However, Christians are able to take comfort in the knowledge that all their sins are forgiven in Christ (1 John 1:9).

Three questions come to mind: First, does that mean it is better not to know truth and to avoid responsibilities? Wouldn't that make us less guilty before God? A person who thinks and lives like that shows a bad spirit, which God knows. He is clearly unconverted and will be condemned for his sin (Matt. 25:24-25, 30). Second, what of the professing Christian who lives in sin, claiming that he is under grace and not under law? Again, we have conclude that he is not truly converted (Rom. 6:22-23; 8:9-10). Third, are there degrees of punishment in hell? We may rightly conclude that there are degrees of punishment in hell, just as there are degrees of reward in heaven (Rev. 22:12; 1 Cor. 3:10-15; 2 Cor. 5:10). However, there is no such place called "purgatory", as taught by the Roman Catholic Church, where sins are punished sufficiently to release the person to heaven.

Q66. What does every sin deserve?
A66. Every sin deserves God's wrath and curse, both in this life and that which is to come[1, 2].

1 Eph. 5:6, Let no one deceive you with empty words, for because of these things the wrath of God comes upon the sons of disobedience.

2 Psalm 11:6, Upon the wicked He will rain coals; fire and brimstone and a burning wind *shall be* the portion of their cup.

Comments

The wrath of God is His holy displeasure against sin. His curse is the eternal punishment which He has pronounced against sin. The breaking of any point of the law is the breaking of the whole of God's perfect law (James 2:10). Since we have not kept God's law perfectly, we are guilty before Him. We deserve eternal damnation from the eternal and perfect God. Unless a person's sins have been cancelled by the death of Christ, unless he is clothed in Christ's righteousness, he will perish under God's wrath and curse (Acts 2:38; Rom. 3:21-26).

God's longsuffering is such that He often warns sinners so that they might repent (Luke 13:1-5). There are times when He punishes by taking away lives (Acts 5:1-11; 1 Cor. 11:30). Not all sufferings and loss of lives are due to particular sins committed by the individuals concerned (cf. Job 1:1, 12). Those who suffer should engage in self-examination to see what the Lord is saying to them, but it is not for others to make judgement about their sufferings (cf. Job 42:7-8).

Part III

THE CHRISTIAN LIFE

Fifteen

THE WAY TO BE SAVED

Q67[1]. **What way of escape has God revealed to sinners that they may be saved from His wrath and curse due to them for their sin?**
A67. God has revealed to sinners the gospel of His Son, Jesus Christ, as the only way of salvation from their sin[1, 2].

1 Rom. 1:16, For I am not ashamed of the gospel of Christ, for it is the power of God to salvation for everyone who believes, for the Jew first and also for the Greek.

2 Acts 4:12, Nor is there salvation in any other, for there is no other name under heaven given among men by which we must be saved.

Comments

God's revealed way of salvation is by the hearing of the gospel (Rom. 10:17; 1 Pet. 1:22-23). The gospel is a distinct message that may be summarized as "Jesus Christ and Him crucified" (1 Cor. 2:2). It is found throughout the Bible (Luke 24:27, 44). It is to be preached with the aim of winning souls to Christ (Matt. 28:18-20; Acts 20:20-21; Rom. 10:14, 17). Once souls are saved, they need "the whole

---

[1]The question on the way of salvation has been divided into two, viz. Qs. 67 and 68.

counsel of God" to build them up in the faith (Acts 20:27; Eph. 4:11-16). In other words, they need systematic teaching of the Bible so that "the faith" may be established in them (Jude 3; 2 Pet. 3:18).

We must ensure that the gospel is not perverted by taking away from, adding to, or distorting, its contents. We have noted in Section 7 ("The Spirit's Work In Salvation") that the Roman Catholics err by *addition* to the gospel, teaching that God saves with man's co-operation, by the use of the sacraments of the mass, confession of sins to the priest, baptism, etc.; the Modernists err by *subtraction* from the gospel, teaching that man can be saved by his own power, without the need of the supernatural work of the Holy Spirit; and that the Arminians err by *distortion* of the gospel, teaching that the Holy Spirit works in man only if he first repents and believes. The apostle Paul condemns all who pervert the gospel (Gal. 1:8-9).

Among Reformed preachers, there has been a tendency to either *maximalism* or *minimalism* in gospel preaching. Maximalism is the tendency to be all-encompassing in content, approach and outlook. When applied to gospel preaching, it is claimed that every time the word of God is expounded, the gospel is being preached. The effect of maximalism is to blur the distinctiveness of the gospel message and, therefore, the distinctiveness of gospel preaching. Minimalism has the opposite tendency of reducing everything to its bare essentials. In gospel preaching, minimalism tends to oversimplify the content, limit its scope, and under-estimate the power of the Holy Spirit in converting sinners. Maximalists tend to emphasize teaching at the expense of gospel proclamation, while minimalists tend to emphasize gospel proclamation at the expense of building up believers in "the faith".

Q68. What does God, in His gospel, require of sinners that they may be saved?
A68.[2] God, in His gospel, requires of sinners repentance to life and faith in Jesus Christ that they may escape His wrath due for their sin, and be saved[1, 2].

---

[2]We have placed repentance before faith, as required by the order of logic and the two Bible references used. The questions following are arranged according to this order. Also, we have made the slight alteration from "repentance unto life" of

15. THE WAY TO BE SAVED

1 Acts 20:21, Testifying to Jews, and also to Greeks, repentance toward God and faith toward our Lord Jesus Christ.

2 Acts 2:37-38, Now when they heard *this*, they were cut to the heart, and said to Peter and the rest of the apostles, "Men *and* brethren, what shall we do?" Then Peter said to them, "Repent, and let every one of you be baptized in the name of Jesus Christ for the remission of sins; and you shall receive the gift of the Holy Spirit."

Comments

The gospel that is heard must be responded to by repentance and faith. Together, repentance and faith constitute conversion. They are two sides of the same coin. When there is true repentance, there will be genuine faith, and *vice versa*. Conversion may be sudden, or it may be drawn out. It may be dramatic, or it may be mild (cf. Saul and the Ethiopian eunuch in Acts 8 & 9). Although repentance and faith are the gifts of God (see later), it is the responsibility of the sinner to repent and believe (Acts 2:37-38). The inability of man to believe is not to be confused with the moral responsibility to believe. The inability of man to stop sinning does not nullify his responsibility for his sins. It is not for the sinner to know whether or not he is chosen by God for salvation, but it is his responsibility to turn from sin and to call out to God for mercy (Mark 9:24).

Repentance and faith do not contribute to salvation which already is complete in Jesus Christ (Col. 2:10; 4:12). They are the means needed to receive the salvation that is given freely by God to undeserving sinners. The call to repentance and faith is part and parcel of gospel preaching. **Hyper-Calvinism** is the error of believing in the sovereignty of God while denying the responsibility of man to respond in repentance and faith to the gospel. **Arminianism** is the error of emphasizing the ability of man to respond to the gospel at the expense of the sovereignty of God in salvation. The true Calvinist

---

the KJV Bible to "repentance to life" of the NKJV (cf. Acts 11:18). The relevant scriptures show that "the means of grace" are to be distinguished from "the means of salvation", and are therefore left out of the answer of this question. Keach's Catechism follows the Shorter Catechism by including "the means of grace" in the answer.

would follow the teaching of the Bible to press home the responsibility of the sinner to respond in repentance and faith, while clearly teaching that God alone, in Christ, saves. The gospel is to be preach to all alike, with the call to everyone to repent and believe. This has been called "the free offer of the gospel", which some people are unhappy with because it is claimed that it implies insincerity on the part of God, who never truly intended to save those who are not the elect.

Q69. What is repentance to life?
A69.[3] Repentance to life is a saving grace[1], whereby a sinner, with grief and hatred of his sin, turns from it to God[2, 3], with full purpose to strive after new obedience[4, 5].

1 Acts 11:18, When they heard these things they became silent; and they glorified God, saying, "Then God has also granted to the Gentiles repentance to life."

2 Jer. 31:18-19, I have surely heard Ephraim bemoaning himself: 'You have chastised me, and I was chastised, like an untrained bull; restore me, and I will return, for You *are* the LORD my God. Surely, after my turning, I repented; and after I was instructed, I struck myself on the thigh; I was ashamed, yes, even humiliated, because I bore the reproach of my youth.'

3 2 Cor. 7:10-11, For godly sorrow produces repentance *leading* to salvation, not to be regretted; but the sorrow of the world produces death. For observe this very thing, that you sorrowed in a godly manner: what diligence it produced in you, *what clearing of yourselves, what* indignation, *what* fear, *what* vehement desire, *what* zeal, *what* vindication! In all *things* you proved yourselves to be clear in this matter.

---

[3]The answer of this question is couched in a similar way to that of the next question, omitting "out of a true sense of his sin, and apprehension of the mercy of God in Christ". Instead of the original phrase, "with full purpose of, and endeavour after, new obedience", we have followed Spurgeon's "with full purpose to strive after new obedience".

15. THE WAY TO BE SAVED

4 Psalm 119:59, I thought about my ways, and turned my feet to Your testimonies.

5 Rom. 6:18, And having been set free from sin, you became slaves of righteousness.

Comments

True repentance involves all three faculties of the human personality – the mind, the heart, and the will (cf. Rom. 6:17: 2 Tim. 1:7). In true repentance, the mind is enlightened concerning the mercy of God in Christ (Jer. 31:18-19), the heart is convicted of guilt and shame due to sins (Joel 2:12-13; Luke 18:13), and the will resolves to turn from rebellion against God to submission to Him (1 Thess. 1:9; Rom. 6:17-18). Such repentance is the gift of God (Acts 11:18). Although the truly repentant person does not become perfect in this life, he strives to obey God (Rom. 6:18). He does not merely abstain from past sins, but strives to live a righteous life (2 Pet. 3:18; Gal. 5:19-26).

There is a repentance that is of the world, that does not save (2 Cor. 7:10-11). It consists of remorse over sins, hurt pride, guilt, and shame at being found out, but there is no turning to God for mercy and, therefore, no trusting in Christ for salvation. The remorse experienced by Judas Iscariot was of this kind (Matt. 27:3-5; Acts 1:15-19).

Q70. What is faith in Jesus Christ?
A70.[4] **Faith in Jesus Christ is a saving grace**[1]**, whereby a sinner receives**[2] **and rests upon Him alone for salvation**[3]**, as He is set forth in the gospel**[4]**.**

---

[4]Following C. H. Spurgeon, we have used the expression "set forth" instead of "offered to us", in view of the continuing controversy over the use of the latter. We have changed "whereby we receive and rest" to "whereby a sinner receives and rests". Also, we have changed the first and last references, which originally were Heb. 10:39 and Isa. 33:22, respectively.

1 Eph. 2:8-9, For by grace you have been saved through faith, and that not of yourselves; *it is* the gift of God, not of works, lest anyone should boast.

2 John 1:12, But as many as received Him, to them He gave the right to become children of God, to those who believe in His name.

3 Phil. 3:9, And be found in Him, not having my own righteousness, which *is* from the law, but that which *is* through faith in Christ, the righteousness which is from God by faith.

4 Rom. 10:14, 17, How then shall they call on Him in whom they have not believed? And how shall they believe in Him of whom they have not heard? And how shall they hear without a preacher? So then faith *comes* by hearing, and hearing by the word of God.

Comments

God's grace is His favour or kindness shown to undeserving people. The "common grace" of God is shown to all people for their good and comfort in this world, but it does not end in salvation (Matt. 5:44-45; Psalm 50:10-11, 22-23). The "saving grace" of God is shown to the elect, and leads to salvation (Eph. 2:8-9). Just as true repentance is a saving grace, so also true faith in Christ is a saving grace. They are the gifts of God. The biblical teaching of "salvation by grace, through faith, in Christ alone", otherwise described as "justification by faith, in Christ alone" (Eph. 2:8-9: Rom. 5:1-2) stands in contrast to all systems of "salvation by works" taught in other religions as well as such groups as the Roman Catholics and the Churches of Christ. The Roman Catholics believe in justification by faith in Christ *plus* the keeping of the sacraments of the mass, baptism, penance, etc. Many of the Churches of Christ (followers of Alexander Campbell) believe in justification by faith in Christ *plus* baptism by immersion.

True faith is shown by: (i) believing in Christ as the Saviour; (ii) trusting in His death on the cross for reconciliation with God (including atonement for sins and imputed righteousness for acceptance before God); and (iii) spiritual growth (Matt. 13:23; John 15:5-6; 2 Pet. 3:18). Spiritual growth is seen in the understanding of the truth, obedience to the truth, and usefulness in God's service

15. THE WAY TO BE SAVED

(2 Pet. 3:18; Heb. 5:13-14). Believing in "another Jesus", different from the one taught in the Bible, cannot save anyone (2 Cor. 11:3-5 cf. Gal. 1:8-9). Similarly, believing in a god different from the trinitarian God of the Bible cannot save anyone. (See Q20 and Q44.)

Sixteen

THE MEANS OF GRACE

Q71. What are the outward and ordinary means whereby the Holy Spirit communicates to us the benefits of redemption?
A71.[1] The outward and ordinary means whereby the Holy Spirit communicates to us the benefits of Christ's redemption are the word[1,2], by which souls are saved and edified; together with baptism, the Lord's Supper, and prayer, by which believers are further edified in their faith[3].

1. James 1:18, Of His own will He brought us forth by the word of truth, that we might be a kind of firstfruits of His creatures.

2. Matt. 4:4, But He answered and said, "It is written, *'Man shall not live by bread alone, but by every word that proceeds from the mouth of God.'*"

3. Acts 2:41-42, Then those who gladly received his word were baptized; and that day about three thousand souls were added *to them*. And they continued steadfastly in the apostles' doctrine and fellowship, in the breaking of bread, and in prayers.

---

[1] We have modelled the answer after Spurgeon's, leaving out meditation since it is related to the use of the word, replacing "souls are begotten to spiritual life" with "souls are saved and edified", and replacing "most holy faith" with "faith", although the former expression is found in Jude 20.

Comments

When a person truly repents of his sin and believes in Jesus Christ, his salvation is complete and secure (Col. 2:10; John 10:28; Rom. 8:38-39). From another point of view, it can be said that his salvation is not yet complete, or fully accomplished. There is the past, present, and future aspects to his salvation. He has been saved through faith in Christ, he is being saved while in this life (Phil. 2:12-13), and he will be saved when Christ returns to judge the world (1 Pet. 1:5). God uses means to sustain the faith of His people so that they are preserved to the end. These are "the means of grace".

From Q29, we learn that the *agent* who applies the redemption to God's elect is the Holy Spirit, while the *manner* by which He applies the redemption is by working repentance and faith, and so uniting them to Christ. But what are the *means* used to sustain faith? The means used by the Holy Spirit are three: (i) the word; (ii) the special ordinances of baptism and the Lord's Supper; and (iii) prayer. These are all "ordinances", or things which God has ordained. They all are *outward* means in that they are visible and involve the effort of believers. They are *ordinary* means, unlike tongue-speaking, healing and miracles, which are extraordinary workings of the Holy Spirit that have been withdrawn by God with the passing of the apostles and the completion of Scripture. By extension, other beneficial activities often are regarded as means of grace as well, e.g. fellowship, service to God, fasting, singing of hymns, psalms and spiritual songs, etc.

Q72. How is the word made effectual to salvation?
A72.[2] The Spirit of God makes the reading[1, 2], but especially the preaching of the word[3, 4], an effectual means of convicting and converting sinners[5, 6], and of building them up in holiness and comfort[7, 8], through faith to salvation[9, 10].

---

[2]We have followed Spurgeon in using the word "convicting" instead of "convincing", in the answer. The Scripture references have been changed. We have left out the next question of the original Catechism, "How is the word to be read and heard that it may become effectual to salvation?"

16. THE MEANS OF GRACE

1 Neh. 8:8, So they read distinctly from the book, in the Law of God; and they gave the sense, and helped *them* to understand the reading.

2 1 Tim. 4:13, 16, Till I come, give attention to reading, to exhortation, to doctrine. Take heed to yourself and to the doctrine. Continue in them, for in doing this you will save both yourself and those who hear you.

3 1 Cor. 1:21, For since, in the wisdom of God, the world through wisdom did not know God, it pleased God through the foolishness of the message preached to save those who believe.

4 Rom. 10:17, So then faith *comes* by hearing, and hearing by the word of God.

5 Psalm 19:7, The law of the LORD *is* perfect, converting the soul; the testimony of the LORD *is* sure, making wise the simple.

6 1 Cor. 14:24-25, But if all prophesy, and an unbeliever or an uninformed person comes in, he is convinced by all, he is convicted by all. And thus the secrets of his heart are revealed; and so, falling down on *his* face, he will worship God and report that God is truly among you.

7 Acts 20:32, So now, brethren, I commend you to God and to the word of His grace, which is able to build you up and give you an inheritance among all those who are sanctified.

8 Rom. 15:4, For whatever things were written before were written for our learning, that we through the patience and comfort of the Scriptures might have hope.

9 Matt. 4:4, But He answered and said, *"It is written, 'Man shall not live by bread alone, but by every word that proceeds from the mouth of God.'"*

10 Eph. 5:26, That He might sanctify and cleanse her with the washing of water by the word.

Comments

The Spirit may use the reading the word of God alone to save, but His usual method is to use the hearing of the preached word (Rom. 10:17; Acts 8:30-35). The gospel of "Jesus Christ and Him crucified" should constitute the primary essence of preaching to unconverted people (1 Cor. 2:2; Acts 20:20-21). Preachers must seek out people and gain a hearing from them (Matt. 28:18-20; Acts 17:16-17). Radio ministry and the distribution of tracts, books, and even recorded messages are useful aids in outreach, but God desires to honour the meeting of souls to minister life to others (cf. Matt. 18:20).

Just as salvation comes mainly by hearing the preached word, so also the faith of believers need to be sustained and preserved by the hearing of the preached word (Matt. 4:4; Eph. 5:26). Believers should be integrated into the life of the local church, and meet regularly with other believers around God's word (Acts 2:42, 46-47; Heb. 10:24-25). The word needs to be heard, understood, obeyed, and meditated upon to benefit the believer. Meditation is a neglected spiritual discipline among Christians (cf. Josh. 1:8; Psalms 1:2; 63:6; Phil. 4:8). The word of God is used by the Spirit to minister strength and comfort to believers in times of trial and crisis (Acts 20:32; Rom. 15:4).

Q73. How do baptism and the Lord's Supper become spiritually helpful?
A73. Baptism and the Lord's Supper become spiritually helpful, not from any virtue in them, or in him who administers them[1], but only by the blessing of Christ[2,3], and the working of the Spirit in those who by faith receive them[4].

1. 1 Cor. 3:6-7, I planted, Apollos watered, but God gave the increase. So then neither he who plants is anything, nor he who waters, but God who gives the increase.

2. 1 Pet. 3:21, There is also an antitype which now saves us—baptism (not the removal of the filth of the flesh, but the answer of a good conscience toward God), through the resurrection of Jesus Christ.

3 1 Cor. 11:29, For he who eats and drinks in an unworthy manner eats and drinks judgment to himself, not discerning the Lord's body.

4 1 Cor. 12:13, For by one Spirit we were all baptized into one body—whether Jews or Greeks, whether slaves or free—and have all been made to drink into one Spirit.

Comments

The Roman Catholic Church teaches that sacraments are "efficacious signs of grace, instituted by Christ and entrusted to the Church, by which divine life is dispensed to us" (RC Catechism). It is claimed that there are seven sacraments, viz. baptism, confirmation, penance, matrimony, the mass, ordination, and extreme unction. The churches of the Reformation claim only two, namely baptism and the Lord's Supper. Most Baptists have difficulty retaining the name of "sacraments" and prefer instead the word "ordinances", i.e. those things ordained by God. To distinguish baptism and the Lord's Supper from other ordinances like the word of God and prayer, Keach's Catechism calls them "holy ordinances". For our purpose, we will refer to baptism and the Lord's Supper as "special ordinances". They are special in that: (i) the Lord specifically commanded them; (ii) they are to be kept to the end of the age; and (iii) they are signs of inward spiritual realities (Matt. 28:18-20; 1 Cor. 11:23-26; Rom. 6:3-6; 1 Cor. 10:17).

Baptism and the Lord's Supper are the special ordinances of the local church. Only a covenanted community of God's people carry out these ordinances. Since they are enacted proclamations of the gospel, recognized preachers or those delegated by them may administer these ordinances (John 4:2). Since they are signs of spiritual realities, any deficiency in carrying out these signs will not affect the realities they represent (1 Cor. 1:14-17). Judas turned out to be an apostate, but that did not nullify the baptism he carried out on behalf of the Lord. However, believers would want to ensure that these ordinances are carried out scripturally. For baptism to be valid, it must have been carried out: (i) by a true church; (ii) by a person authorized by the church; (iii) on a person who is a believer; (iv) in the names of the Father, the Son, and the Holy Spirit; and (v) by complete immersion. For the Lord's Supper to be valid, it must be carried out: (i) by a true church; (ii) by a person authorized by the church; (iii) for those who are believers; and (iv) for those who are not under discipline in any church.

Q74.[3] How does prayer become spiritually helpful?
A74. Prayer becomes spiritually helpful, not from any virtue in it, or in him who engages in it[1, 2], but only by the blessing of Christ[3], and the working of the Spirit in the one who prays[4, 5].

1 Matt. 6:5, 7, And when you pray, you shall not be like the hypocrites. For they love to pray standing in the synagogues and on the corners of the streets, that they may be seen by men. Assuredly, I say to you, they have their reward. And when you pray, do not use vain repetitions as the heathen *do*. For they think that they will be heard for their many words.

2 Dan. 9:18, O my God, incline Your ear and hear; open Your eyes and see our desolations, and the city which is called by Your name; for we do not present our supplications before You because of our righteous deeds, but because of Your great mercies.

3 John 14:13-14, And whatever you ask in My name, that I will do, that the Father may be glorified in the Son. If you ask anything in My name, I will do *it*.

4 Acts 4:31; And when they had prayed, the place where they were assembled together was shaken; and they were all filled with the Holy Spirit, and they spoke the word of God with boldness.

5 Acts 9:11, So the Lord *said* to him, "Arise and go to the street called Straight, and inquire at the house of Judas for *one* called Saul of Tarsus, for behold, he is praying."

---

[3]This question has been added for completeness, the answer of which is couched in the same form as that of the previous question.

16. THE MEANS OF GRACE

Comments

Prayer is an indication of spiritual life, just as breathing is an indication of physical life (Rom. 8:14-15). The Lord taught His disciples to pray. There are many examples of prayer in the Bible. It is taken for granted in the Bible that all believers will pray (Matt. 6:5). The mere act of prayer does not impart spiritual good to the person. The Pharisees uttered prayers but were not approved by the Lord (Matt. 6:5). Daniel understood that it was not due to his own righteousness that God heard his prayer (Dan. 9:18). For there to be spiritual good, the Lord must bless, by the working of the Spirit, those who pray.

Prayer is to be carried out individually (Mark 1:35; 6:46) as well as corporately (Acts 4:31). When appropriate, it may be accompanied by fasting. Just as meditation is a neglected spiritual discipline, so also is fasting among Christians. Fasting is to be done in conjunction with prayer, while prayer may be carried out without fasting. The Lord expects His disciples to engage in voluntary fasting (Matt. 6:16 cf. 5; Mark 9:29; Acts 10:4, 30; 9-10). The blessedness of walking in close communion with the Lord should be sought by all God's people – in prayer, and in attending to the other means of grace.

Seventeen

THE SPECIAL ORDINANCES

Q75. What is baptism?
A75.[1] Baptism is a special ordinance of the New Testament, instituted by Jesus Christ[1], to be to the person baptised, a sign of his spiritual union with Him – in His death, burial and resurrection[2, 3] – to walk in newness of life[4, 5].

1. Matt. 28:19, Go therefore and make disciples of all the nations, baptizing them in the name of the Father and of the Son and of the Holy Spirit.

2. Rom. 6:3, Or do you not know that as many of us as were baptized into Christ Jesus were baptized into His death?

3. Col. 2:12, Buried with Him in baptism, in which you also were raised with *Him* through faith in the working of God, who raised Him from the dead.

4. Rom. 6:4-5, Therefore we were buried with Him through baptism into death, that just as Christ was raised from the dead by the glory of the Father, even so we also should walk in newness of life. For if we have been united together in the likeness of His death, certainly we also shall be *in the likeness* of *His* resurrection.

---

[1] The answer, which is based on Spurgeon's, has been simplified.

5 Gal. 3:27, For as many of you as were baptized into Christ have put on Christ.

Comments

This is one of the two "special ordinances" of the church, different from hearing the word and prayer, in that they were instituted by Christ to represent and apply to believers the benefits of the new covenant by visible and outward signs. The paedobaptists regard these as not only signs, but also seals, whereas the Bible teaches that it is the Holy Spirit who is the seal of our salvation (Eph. 1:13; 4:30). In Romans 4:11, circumcision was a sign which, to Abraham in particular, was also a seal (authentication) of the righteousness imputed to him before his circumcision.

A physical and visible sign points to an internal and spiritual reality. Baptism signifies our union with Christ in His death, burial and resurrection. It is also a declaration that we desire to walk with Christ in newness of life.

Q76. To whom is baptism to be administered?
A76.[2] Baptism is to be administered to all those who credibly profess repentance towards God[1], and faith in our Lord Jesus Christ[2, 3], and to none other.

1 Acts 2:38, 41, Then Peter said to them, "Repent, and let every one of you be baptized in the name of Jesus Christ for the remission of sins; and you shall receive the gift of the Holy Spirit." Then those who gladly received his word were baptized; and that day about three thousand souls were added *to them.*

2 Mark 16:16, He who believes and is baptized will be saved; but he who does not believe will be condemned.

3 Acts 8:12, But when they believed Philip as he preached the things concerning the kingdom of God and the name of Jesus Christ, both men and women were baptized.

---

[2]The word "credibly" replaces "actually".

17. THE SPECIAL ORDINANCES

Comments

Only converted people, i.e. those who have repented and believed, are to be baptised. Regardless of whether you are from a pagan background or a Christian background, you should get baptised when converted. Baptism does not save, for salvation is "by grace, through faith, in Christ alone" (Eph. 2:8-9; Rom. 10:17 cf. Luke 23:42-43). A saved person would want to be baptised in obedience to the Lord's command (Matt. 28:18-20; Acts 2:38, 41).

While baptism should take place as closely as possible to the time of conversion, only those who show a credible profession of faith should be baptised. In the New Testament, professing believers were baptised immediately because: (i) the apostles had the gift of discernment to determine who were saved (Acts 5:1-11); (ii) it was a time of persecution when discipleship was very costly (Acts 8:1-3); (iii) the people met often such that there were more opportunities to know one another (Acts 2:46). Today, a credible profession of faith may be determined from the person's understanding of the gospel, experience of conversion, obedience to the Lord, and commitment to God's people. Practically, all these can be assessed only when the person attends church regularly, gets to know others, and shares about his life.

Q77. Are the infants of professing believers to be baptised?
A77. The infants of professing believers are not to be baptised because there is neither command, example, nor clear inference in the Holy Scriptures for their baptism[1-3].

1 2 Tim. 3:16-17, All Scripture *is* given by inspiration of God, and *is* profitable for doctrine, for reproof, for correction, for instruction in righteousness, that the man of God may be complete, thoroughly equipped for every good work.

2 Rev. 22:18-19, For I testify to everyone who hears the words of the prophecy of this book: If anyone adds to these things, God will add to him the plagues that are written in this book; and if anyone takes away from the words of the book of this prophecy,

God shall take away his part from the Book of Life, from the holy city, and *from* the things which are written in this book.

3 Prov. 30:6, Do not add to His words, lest He rebuke you, and you be found a liar.

Comments

Christians who practise infant sprinkling are known as *paedobaptists*. They acknowledge that there is no command for, or example of, infant baptism in the Bible, but argue that infant baptism is taught indirectly. For example, they claim that "the promises of God" extend to their children based on such passages as Acts 2:39, 1 Cor. 7:14; Acts 16:15, 31. These passages, however, speak of those who believe, and not of infants (Acts 2:39 cf. Matt. 28:18-20; Acts 16:32, 34; 1 Cor. 1:16 cf. 16:15). The Acts 2:39 passage is about the specific promise of receiving the Holy Spirit, without which none will be saved (cf. Rom. 8:9). It applies to all believers – "as many as the Lord our God will call". Paedobaptists also claim that children of believers are "under the covenant of grace" and should receive the covenant sign of baptism in the same way that infants in the Old Testament were circumcised. However, the Bible shows that the covenant of grace encompasses those capable of making a profession of faith, not infants (Heb. 8:10-12). Of course, elect infants who die in infancy and the mentally handicapped are also saved by Christ's death, but that is not our concern here. Baptism is a new sign of the new covenant. Circumcision in the Old Testament was a type of regeneration in Christ, not of baptism (Col. 2:11-12). In theology, a "type" cannot be fulfilled by an "anti-type" that is another external sign, but by a spiritual reality.

We do not regard infant baptism as biblical baptism. A person who has been "baptised" as an infant should consider getting baptised when converted, "to fulfill all righteousness", i.e. to do what is right and pleasing before God (Matt. 3:15).

Q78. How is baptism rightly administered?
A78.[3] Baptism is rightly administered by complete immersion

17. THE SPECIAL ORDINANCES

of the person in water[1, 2], in the name of the Father, and of the Son, and of the Holy Spirit[3], and by one who is authorized by the Lord[4, 5].

1 Matt. 3:16, When He had been baptized, Jesus came up immediately from the water; and behold, the heavens were opened to Him, and He saw the Spirit of God descending like a dove and alighting upon Him.

2 John 3:23, Now John also was baptizing in Aenon near Salim, because there was much water there. And they came and were baptized.

3 Matt. 28:19-20, "Go therefore and make disciples of all the nations, baptizing them in the name of the Father and of the Son and of the Holy Spirit, teaching them to observe all things that I have commanded you; and lo, I am with you always, *even* to the end of the age." Amen.

4 John 4:1-2, Therefore, when the Lord knew that the Pharisees had heard that Jesus made and baptized more disciples than John (though Jesus Himself did not baptize, but His disciples).

5 Acts 8:38-39, So he commanded the chariot to stand still. And both Philip and the eunuch went down into the water, and he baptized him. Now when they came up out of the water, the Spirit of the Lord caught Philip away, so that the eunuch saw him no more; and he went on his way rejoicing.

Comments

The word translated "baptism" is derived from the Greek word "baptizo", meaning "to dip, to immerse, to submerge". It is different from "rhantizo" which means "to sprinkle". The examples of baptism in the Bible support immersion, since both the person baptised and the person baptising had to enter much water (Matt. 3:16; John 3:23; Acts 8:36, 38-39). Furthermore, only immersion is capable of visibly representing death, burial and resurrection (Rom. 6:4).

---

[3]We have added the last clause to the answer.

We reject sprinkling, pouring, and partial dipping of the body as the biblical way of baptizing. It is better not to baptize a bed-ridden, critically sick, believer than to replace biblical baptism with sprinkling or pouring of water. The thief who believed in the Lord while dying on the cross was not baptized (Luke 23:42-43). The water used in baptism may be still or running, clear or muddy, and fresh or salty.

Baptism is to be performed in the names of the three Persons of the Godhead. The instances of baptism done "in the name of the Lord" in Acts 8:16; 10:48 and 19:5 simply means "after believing in the Lord". They are not a description of *how* baptism was carried out, but *why* baptism was carried out. Since the special ordinances are visual proclamations of Christ, ministers of the gospel have a responsibility to administer them. That responsibility, which is from the Lord through the church, may be delegated to others (John 4:1-2).

Q79. What is the Lord's Supper?
A79.[4] The Lord's Supper is a special ordinance of the New Testament, instituted by Jesus Christ[1], to be to the persons partaking, a sign of their spiritual union with Him – by faith receiving His body and blood symbolized in the bread and cup[2] – for their spiritual nourishment and growth in grace[3, 4].

1   1 Cor. 11:23-26, For I received from the Lord that which I also delivered to you: that the Lord Jesus on the *same* night in which He was betrayed took bread; and when He had given thanks, He broke *it* and said, "Take, eat; this is My body which is broken for you; do this in remembrance of Me." In the same manner *He* also *took* the cup after supper, saying, "This cup is the new covenant in My blood. This do, as often as you drink *it*, in remembrance of Me." For as often as you eat this bread and drink this cup, you proclaim the Lord's death till He comes.

---

[4]The answer has been completely re-written to conform with the answer of Q75, but couched in the plural form. Also, "cup" replaces "wine".

17. THE SPECIAL ORDINANCES

2 1 Cor. 10:16, The cup of blessing which we bless, is it not the communion of the blood of Christ? The bread which we break, is it not the communion of the body of Christ?

3 John 6:53-57, Then Jesus said to them, "Most assuredly, I say to you, unless you eat the flesh of the Son of Man and drink His blood, you have no life in you. Whoever eats My flesh and drinks My blood has eternal life, and I will raise him up at the last day. For My flesh is food indeed, and My blood is drink indeed. He who eats My flesh and drinks My blood abides in Me, and I in him. As the living Father sent Me, and I live because of the Father, so he who feeds on Me will live because of Me."

4 John 15:5, I am the vine, you *are* the branches. He who abides in Me, and I in him, bears much fruit; for without Me you can do nothing.

Comments

Just as baptism was given to the church, so also the Lord's Supper (Matt. 28:18-20; 1 Cor. 11:23). It is abused when carried out for the bride and groom during a wedding, or by Christian students staying in a hostel. The normal order is that baptism should precede the Lord's Supper (Acts 2:41-42). In baptism, the subject is passive but resolves to actively walk in obedience with the Lord. In the Lord's Supper, the subject actively takes the elements but is passive in receiving spiritual nourishment from the Lord.

The bread used may be leavened or unleavened, flat or round, sweet or plain. The word used is "bread", not "wafer" (although the Chinese Bible translates it as "wafer" or "biscuit"). The Passover of the Old Testament was a "type" of the regenerating work of Christ in sinners, not of the Lord's Supper (1 Cor. 5:7). The Bible uses the word "cup" (1 Cor. 10:16; 11:25) and the expression "the fruit of the vine" (Matt. 26:29; Mark 14:25; Luke 22:18). The latter is a general term covering grape juice that is fresh as well as fermented (i.e. wine). Its deliberate usage with regard to the Lord's Supper show that we should be careful about using wine, and should feel free to use unfermented fruit juice. Focussing too much on the details of the ordinances, and missing out on what are being symbolized, will lead to the the errors of the Pharisees – legalism and quibbling over details. Note that the symbolism of "one bread" is better than the cut-up pieces of bread used in many churches (1 Cor. 10:17 cf. Luke 22:19). On the other hand, there is no need for the "one cup" used in many churches because, at the institution of the Lord's Supper, the content of the cup was divided (Luke 22:20 cf. 17).

Q80. What is required for the worthy receiving of the Lord's Supper?
A80.[5] **Those receiving the Lord's Supper must examine themselves, making sure that they have the understanding to discern the Lord's body[1], the faith to feed upon Him[2], and the life of repentance, love, and new obedience[3-5], lest coming unworthily, they eat and drink judgment to themselves[6].**

1. 1 Cor. 11:28-29, But let a man examine himself, and so let him eat of the bread and drink of the cup. For he who eats and drinks in an unworthy manner eats and drinks judgment to himself, not discerning the Lord's body.

2. 2 Cor. 13:5, Examine yourselves *as to* whether you are in the faith. Test yourselves. Do you not know yourselves, that Jesus Christ is in you?—unless indeed you are disqualified.

3. 1 Cor. 11:31, For if we would judge ourselves, we would not be judged.

4. 1 Cor. 11:18-20, For first of all, when you come together as a church, I hear that there are divisions among you, and in part I believe it. For there must also be factions among you, that those who are approved may be recognized among you. Therefore when you come together in one place, it is not to eat the Lord's Supper.

5. 1 Cor. 5:8, Therefore let us keep the feast, not with old leaven, nor with the leaven of malice and wickedness, but with the unleavened *bread* of sincerity and truth.

---

[5]We have considerably altered the form of the answer while retaining the substance.

17. THE SPECIAL ORDINANCES

6 1 Cor. 11:27, 29, Therefore whoever eats this bread or drinks *this* cup of the Lord in an unworthy manner will be guilty of the body and blood of the Lord. For he who eats and drinks in an unworthy manner eats and drinks judgment to himself, not discerning the Lord's body.

Comments

Some churches practice "open communion", allowing all and sundry to partake. Some practise "closed communion", allowing only members of the church, or of the same denomination, to partake. Our church practise "restricted communion", i.e. allowing "baptised believers who are not under discipline in any church", while personally inviting visiting believers of paedobaptist conviction to partake.

To derive spiritual benefit from the Lord's Supper, the mind, the heart, and the will must be engaged – (i) the mind in understanding the broken body and shed blood of Christ; (ii) the heart in trusting in Him; (iii) the will in repentance for past sins, having present love for God's people, and desiring future obedience to Him. The "past, present, and future" is with respect to the Lord's Supper while it is in progress. The Roman Catholic Church teaches "transubstantiation", claiming that the elements turn into real flesh and real blood as they are taken in. The Lutherans believe in "consubstantiation", i.e. that Christ is with, in, or under the elements. We believe that the elements only symbolize the flesh and blood of Christ, while Christ is present spiritually with His gathered people (Matt. 18:19-20).

Eighteen

GOD-CENTRED PRAYER

Q81.[1] What is prayer?
A81. Prayer is the offering up of the desires of the righteous[1] to God[2], for things agreeable to His will[3], in the name of Christ[4], by the help of His Spirit[5], with confession of our sins[6] and thankful acknowledgement of His mercies[7].

1 Prov. 15:8, The sacrifice of the wicked *is* an abomination to the LORD, but the prayer of the upright *is* His delight.

2 Psalm 62:8, Trust in Him at all times, you people; pour out your heart before Him; God *is* a refuge for us.

3 1 John 5:14, Now this is the confidence that we have in Him, that if we ask anything according to His will, He hears us.

4 John 16:23, And in that day you will ask Me nothing. Most assuredly, I say to you, whatever you ask the Father in My name He will give you.

5 Rom. 8:26, Likewise the Spirit also helps in our weaknesses. For we do not know what we should pray for as we ought, but the

---

[1] Spurgeon's Catechism leaves out the section on the Lord's Prayer totally. We have followed the SCBV, making the answer trinitarian, but leaving out "Acceptable" at the beginning of the answer.

Spirit Himself makes intercession for us with groanings which cannot be uttered.

6 Psalm 32:5-6, I acknowledged my sin to You, and my iniquity I have not hidden. I said, "I will confess my transgressions to the LORD," and You forgave the iniquity of my sin. For this cause everyone who is godly shall pray to You in a time when You may be found; surely in a flood of great waters they shall not come near him.

7 Phil. 4:6, Be anxious for nothing, but in everything by prayer and supplication, with thanksgiving, let your requests be made known to God.

Comments

This section shows that prayer should be God-centred, i.e. focused on God, His will, and His glory. Prayer is primarily an an act of worship, not an act of gaining merits before God. It is the presentation of the desires of believers to God, not the attempt of non-believers to gain something from God as they do from pagan deities. This is the chief difference between the prayers of Christians and that of non-Christians and pagans. Many pagan religions, as well as Roman Catholicism, practise reciting certain prayers many times, using a "rosary" (i.e. a chain of beads) to count, to gain merits. True prayer is offered up to God by faith in Jesus Christ.

The true Christian is saved by God's grace, through faith in Christ alone. He has confessed his sins to God and acknowledged His mercy to him, an unworthy sinner. In his life as a believer, he continues to desire for things that are in accordance to God's will. He continues to confess his sins to God and to thank Him for His mercies. All these are made possible only because of the sanctifying work of the Spirit in him. True prayer is different from merely "saying a prayer" (cf. Luke 18:9-14). True prayer arises from a heart that is converted, humble, and thankful (cf. Rom. 8:26-27).

Q82. What rule has God given for the direction of His people in prayer?

18. GOD-CENTRED PRAYER

A82. The whole word of God is of use to direct His people in prayer[1], but the special rule of direction is that pattern of prayer which Christ taught His disciples, commonly called the Lord's Prayer[2].

1. 1 John 5:14, Now this is the confidence that we have in Him, that if we ask anything according to His will, He hears us.

2. Matt. 6:9-13, In this manner, therefore, pray: Our Father in heaven, hallowed be Your name. Your kingdom come. Your will be done on earth as *it is* in heaven. Give us this day our daily bread. And forgive us our debts, as we forgive our debtors. And do not lead us into temptation, but deliver us from the evil one. For Yours is the kingdom and the power and the glory forever. Amen.

Comments

The Lord's Prayer is a pattern, or model, to guide believers. Although it is not wrong, on certain occasions, to recite the Lord's Prayer, it is not intended for this purpose (Matt. 6:9 cf. verse 7). As far as the content and form of our prayers are concerned, the Lord's Prayer teaches us to be: (i) God-centred; (ii) simple; (iii) brief; and (iv) comprehensive.

Other parts of the Bible reinforce the teaching in the Lord's Prayer concerning the attitude and manner of prayer, which should be: (i) reverential; (ii) earnest; (iii) trustful; and (iv) persistent (e.g. Luke 11:5-13; 18:1-8; Dan. 9:18-19).

Q83. What does the preface of the Lord's Prayer teach His disciples?
A83. The preface of the Lord's Prayer, which is, "Our Father in heaven", teaches His disciples to draw near to God, with all holy reverence and confidence, as children to a father, able and ready to help them[1], and that we should pray with[2] and for others[3].

1 Luke 11:13, If you then, being evil, know how to give good gifts to your children, how much more will *your* heavenly Father give the Holy Spirit to those who ask Him!

2 Matt. 18:19-20, Again I say to you that if two of you agree on earth concerning anything that they ask, it will be done for them by My Father in heaven. For where two or three are gathered together in My name, I am there in the midst of them.

3 1 Tim. 2:1-2, Therefore I exhort first of all that supplications, prayers, intercessions, *and* giving of thanks be made for all men, for kings and all who are in authority, that we may lead a quiet and peaceable life in all godliness and reverence.

Comments

A right relationship with God is essential before we can pray acceptably. It is only when we are converted – by grace through faith in Christ alone – that we become children of God (John 1:12-13 cf. John 8:43). Only true believers can call out from their hearts to God, their Father in heaven (Rom. 8:14-15). It is not wrong to teach our children to pray. It is not wrong for non-believers to pray, especially when they are faced with a crisis. God, in His abundance of mercy, might hear them, with the view of drawing them to know Him, through faith in Christ (cf. Mark 9:24; Acts 8:22; 10:30-31).

The prayers of believers are heard by God because of the intercession of Christ the Mediator, who is our High Priest in heaven (Heb. 4:14-16; 10:19-25). God is not so high above us as to be unreachable, nor so much like us as to be powerless to help. As the Father to believers, He hears the prayers of His children. As God in heaven, He is all-powerful and ready to help His children. God takes pleasure in His children drawing near to Him in prayer – both individually and corporately. He desires the prayer of His people to encompass not only personal needs, but also the needs of others.

Q84. What do we pray for in the first petition?
A84. In the first petition, which is "Hallowed be Your name",

18. GOD-CENTRED PRAYER

Christians pray that God would enable them and others to glorify Him in all by which He makes Himself known[1], and that He would dispose all things to His own glory[2].

1 Psalm 67:1-3, God be merciful to us and bless us, *and* cause His face to shine upon us, that Your way may be known on earth, Your salvation among all nations. Let the peoples praise You, O God; let all the peoples praise You.

2 Rom. 11:36, For of Him and through Him and to Him *are* all things, to whom *be* glory forever. Amen.

Comments

The name represents the person and his character. To desire God's name to be "hallowed" is to desire God to be honoured highly. The desire of a Christian is for himself and others to highly honour God in all by which He makes Himself known. God makes Himself known by His word, His people, and His creation. The Christian would want to be faithful to His word, by preaching and teaching it faithfully. He would want the church to reflect His glory – in her membership, government, worship, and service. The necessity of sounding forth warnings against heresies, practising separation from those in serious errors, and exercising corrective discipline must be seen in this light. While we pray for God to send a revival so that many souls will be saved, we must also engage in the reformation of the church so that we will be vessels worthy for God to use (Rom. 9:23; 2 Cor. 4:7).

Q85. What do Christians pray for in the second petition?
A85. In the second petition (which is, "Your kingdom come") Christians pray that Satan's kingdom may be destroyed[1], and that the kingdom of grace may be advanced[2], sinners brought into it[3], and believers kept in it[4], and that the kingdom of glory may be hastened[5].

1 Psalm 68:1, Let God arise, let His enemies be scattered; let those also who hate Him flee before Him.

2 Psalm 51:18, Do good in Your good pleasure to Zion; build the walls of Jerusalem.

3 Matt. 9:37-38, Then He said to His disciples, "The harvest truly *is* plentiful, but the laborers *are* few. Therefore pray the Lord of the harvest to send out laborers into His harvest."

4 John 17:15, 20, I do not pray that You should take them out of the world, but that You should keep them from the evil one. I do not pray for these alone, but also for those who will believe in Me through their word.

5 Rev. 22:20, He who testifies to these things says, "Surely I am coming quickly." Amen. Even so, come, Lord Jesus!

Comments

God's kingdom is His rule in the hearts of men (Luke 17:20; John 18:36). God's glory is seen in the church of Jesus Christ (Eph. 3:21). The salvation of souls and the building up of the church of Jesus Christ are bound up in the Great Commission (Matt. 28:18-20). There is no better way to glorify God than to build up the church of Jesus Christ.

God's kingdom is to be built up, not by imposing Christian values upon the institutions of this world, as the **Theonomy movement** (or **Christian Reconstructionism**) seeks to do, but by spiritual regeneration through the hearing of the gospel (Rom. 10:17: 1 Pet. 1:22-25). It is good for Christians to remember that the kingdom of God is *spiritual, antithetical,* and *eschatological.* Since it is spiritual, it is not to be advanced by the weapons of this world (2 Cor. 10:4). Since it is antithetical, it is to be separate from this world (1 John 2:15 17). Since it is eschatological, it is not to be confused with this temporary world (2 Pet. 3:10-13). Let us live as "strangers and pilgrims on the earth" (Heb. 11:13).

Q86. What do Christians pray for in the third petition?
A86.[2] In the third petition (which is "Your will be done on earth as it is in heaven") Christians pray that God by His grace would

18. GOD-CENTRED PRAYER

make them able and willing to know[1], submit to[2,3], and obey[4] His will in all things, as the angels do in heaven[5].

1. Psalm 119:34, Give me understanding, and I shall keep Your law; indeed, I shall observe it with *my* whole heart.

2. Job 1:21, And he said: "Naked I came from my mother's womb, and naked shall I return there. The LORD gave, and the LORD has taken away; blessed be the name of the LORD."

3. Acts 21:14, So when he would not be persuaded, we ceased, saying, "The will of the Lord be done."

4. Psalm 119:35-36, Make me walk in the path of Your commandments, for I delight in it. Incline my heart to Your testimonies, and not to covetousness.

5. Psalm 103:20-21, Bless the LORD, you His angels, who excel in strength, who do His word, heeding the voice of His word. Bless the LORD, all *you* His hosts, *you* ministers of His, who do His pleasure.

Comments

God's revealed will in the Bible is sufficient for all our needs (2 Tim. 3:16-17; Deut. 29:29). Left to ourselves, remaining sins hinder us from desiring to know, submit to, and obey God's will. We need God's grace to make us able and willing. Teachers are appointed in the church to help us grow spiritually. The chief means of grace is the hearing God's word taught systematically and regularly. If this is not attended to, it is hard to expect spiritual growth (2 Pet. 3:16). It is a mistaken idea to emphasize service at the expense of good teaching. We often hear it said, "If you do not serve, you cannot grow (spiritually)". Service should follow correct and good teaching, not *vice versa* (cf. Heb. 5:12-6:3). Do you seek first the kingdom of God and His righteousness (Matt. 6:33)?

---

[2]The answer has been slightly altered to follow the order of "mind, heart, and will", so that we have "to know, submit to, and obey" instead of "to know, obey, and submit to".

Nineteen

PRAYING FOR NEEDS

Q87. What do Christians pray for in the fourth petition?
A87.[1] In the fourth petition (which is, "Give us this day our daily bread.") Christians pray that they may receive from God a competent portion of the good things of this life, and enjoy His blessing with them[1-3].

1 Prov. 30:8-9, Remove falsehood and lies far from me; give me neither poverty nor riches—feed me with the food allotted to me; lest I be full and deny *You*, and say, "Who *is* the LORD?" or lest I be poor and steal, and profane the name of my God.

2 1 Tim. 4:4-5, For every creature of God *is* good, and nothing is to be refused if it is received with thanksgiving; for it is sanctified by the word of God and prayer.

3 Psalm 90:17, And let the beauty of the LORD our God be upon us, and establish the work of our hands for us; yes, establish the work of our hands.

---

[1]The phrase, "of God's free gift they may receive a competent portion", has been changed to, "they may receive from God a competent portion".

Comments

Three points may be noted. Firstly, "daily bread" speaks of our basic needs. What we *want* may not be what we *need*. We do not pray merely for a supply of needs to barely survive but to live a reasonably comfortable life. When God blesses with abundance, we must be careful not to become proud. Nebuchadnezzar was struck low when he claimed credit for his successes (Dan. 4:28-36). Abraham was rich, but was not drawn away by his riches (Gen. 14:23; 22:21). Jacob acknowledged God's goodness for his riches (Gen. 32:10). It may be difficult for a rich man to enter the kingdom of God, but it is never impossible (cf. Matt. 19:24). The dangers of greed and lack of contentment are ever present, with the rich as well as the poor.

Secondly, to pray for our "daily bread" on a day to day basis shows our dependence on God. When studying the eighth commandment, "You shall not steal", we learned that wealth may be given (as a gift or an inheritance), or earned. Some Christians have greater ability than others to generate wealth, for which they must be thankful. It is legitimate and, in fact, a responsibility to use our talents well for God's glory. The danger here is sinful self-confidence, in which God's sovereignty is overlooked and we fail to trust in Him (James 4:13-17).

Thirdly, we desire God's blessing to accompany His provision. This means that we give generously to needs and to further God's kingdom, since "it is more blessed to give than to receive" (Acts 20:35). Christians have always been on the forefront of practical and financial aid in times of disaster and social needs. We do so not to gain merits with God or the praise of man, but because of the consciousness that we are unworthy sinners saved by God's grace. We, therefore, desire to love God with all our being, and to love our neighbour as ourselves (Mark 12:30-31).

Q88. What do Christians pray for in the fifth petition?
A88.[2] In the fifth petition (which is, "And forgive us our debts, as we forgive our debtors") Christians pray that God, for Christ's sake, would freely pardon all their sins[1] because, by His grace,

19. PRAYING FOR NEEDS

they are enabled from the heart to forgive others[2].

1 Psalm 51:1-2, 7, 9, Have mercy upon me, O God, according to Your lovingkindness; according to the multitude of Your tender mercies, blot out my transgressions. Wash me thoroughly from my iniquity, and cleanse me from my sin. Purge me with hyssop, and I shall be clean; wash me, and I shall be whiter than snow. Hide Your face from my sins, and blot out all my iniquities.

2 Mark 11:25-26, And whenever you stand praying, if you have anything against anyone, forgive him, that your Father in heaven may also forgive you your trespasses. But if you do not forgive, neither will your Father in heaven forgive your trespasses.

Comments

An unforgiving heart cripples a Christian in his spiritual growth and service to God more than he realizes. We are here reminded of the necessity of forgiving those who may have badly offended us and caused us much harm and pain. While there are biblical ways of handling offences between Christians, which extend in some measure to offences involving non-Christians, it is not always possible to settle things well (Matt. 18:15-18; 1 Cor. 5:4-5). This is especially so when there is no reciprocal desire for repentance, forgiveness, and reconciliation. It is important that we have a forgiving heart towards those who have caused us offense, knowing that God has freely forgiven us our sins, in Christ (Matt. 18:21-22). The offender will benefit from our forgiveness only if he repents (Luke 17:3-4). Matthew 6:14-15 does not mean that our salvation will be jeopardized by our lack of forgiveness toward others. Rather, it means that those who are saved will want to forgive others. It may be hard to do so but, with God's help, it is possible.

    Justification is a once for all act on the part of God, forgiving us our sins, and treating us as righteous in Jesus Christ, at the point of our conversion. Sanctification, however, is a continual process by which God works in the believer the desire and ability to live a righteous life. A major part of our sanctification is constantly praying to

---

[2]The phrase, "which they are the more readily encouraged to ask", after "pardon all their sins", has been left out.

God for forgiveness of our sins, committed knowingly or unknowingly (Job 1:5; 1 John 1:8-10). In other words, we not only repent of our sins at the beginning of the Christian life, but continually throughout our Christian life. We have the confidence that God will forgive us, for Christ's sake.

Q89. What do Christians pray for in the sixth petition?
A89. In the sixth petition (which is, "And do not lead us into temptation, but deliver us from the evil one") Christians pray that God would either keep them from being tempted to sin[1, 2], or support and deliver them when they are tempted[3, 4].

1 Matt. 26:41, Watch and pray, lest you enter into temptation. The spirit indeed *is* willing, but the flesh *is* weak.

2 Psalm 19:13, Keep back Your servant also from presumptuous *sins*; let them not have dominion over me. Then I shall be blameless, and I shall be innocent of great transgression.

3 1 Cor. 10:13, No temptation has overtaken you except such as is common to man; but God *is* faithful, who will not allow you to be tempted beyond what you are able, but with the temptation will also make the way of escape, that you may be able to bear *it*.

4 John 17:15, I do not pray that You should take them out of the world, but that You should keep them from the evil one.

Comments

The expression, "do not lead us into temptation" is a "litotes", i.e. an affirmation of something by saying its opposite (e.g. Rev. 3:5). The expression means "lead us in the way everlasting" (Psalm 139:24). God does not maliciously lead His children into temptation but, by His sovereign will, He may allow temptation to come to them (cf. Job 1:12; 2:6). Satan is the source of all temptations, with which he aims to destroy believers (John 8:44; 1 Pet. 5:8). God permits such temptations in order: (i) to show forth His glory in the preservation of His people (Job 1:22; 2:10); (ii) to strengthen the faith of His people (Luke 22:32); and (iii) to chastise His wayward children (Heb. 12:3-11; Psalm 66:8-12). To be tempted to sin is not the same as falling into sin. Before one falls into sin, he is drawn away by temptation, i.e. he is troubled by the temptation, which may ensnare or entangle him (James 1:13-15). When ensnared, we have "fallen into temptation" (Matt. 26:41). It is never pleasant to be ensnared by temptation. We are now in danger of sinning – in thought, word and deed – over that temptation.

How do we handle temptations? First, we must avoid temptations. This is where prayer comes in. Temptations are in the world – from the devil – but they need not succeed in tempting God's children. Second, we must flee from the temptation that manages to gain our attention, while resisting the devil (1 Cor. 6:18; 10:14; James 4:7). God always provides a way of escape (1 Cor. 10:13). Third, when entangled with a temptation, take drastic actions of getting out of it by praying urgently while taking definite measures to put an end to that temptation (Rom. 8:13; Col. 3:5). Fourth, if the temptation cannot be removed, watch and pray that you do not succumb to sin (James 1:12; Matt. 26:41). God's grace is sufficient for us (2 Cor. 12:7-10). Over and above all these steps, Christians must be pro-active in strengthening themselves and avoiding occasions of temptation, instead of always fighting a defensive battle. This can be done only by attending to the means of grace, in company with other believers (1 Tim. 6:11; 2 Tim. 2:22).

Q90. What does the conclusion of the Lord's Prayer teach His disciples?
A90.[3] The conclusion of the Lord's Prayer (which is, "For Yours is the kingdom and the power and the glory forever. Amen.") teaches His disciples to take encouragement in prayer from God only[1], and in their prayers to praise and thank Him[2, 3], and in testimony of their desire and assurance to be heard, to say, Amen[4].

---

[3]We have changed "to praise Him" to "to praise and thank Him", while leaving out the phrase following, which is, "ascribing kingdom, power, and glory to Him".

1 Dan. 9:18-19, O my God, incline Your ear and hear; open Your eyes and see our desolations, and the city which is called by Your name; for we do not present our supplications before You because of our righteous deeds, but because of Your great mercies. O Lord, hear! O Lord, forgive! O Lord, listen and act! Do not delay for Your own sake, my God, for Your city and Your people are called by Your name.

2 1 Chron. 29:11-13, Yours, O LORD, *is* the greatness, the power and the glory, the victory and the majesty; for all *that is* in heaven and in earth *is Yours*; Yours *is* the kingdom, O LORD, and You are exalted as head over all. Both riches and honor *come* from You, and You reign over all. In Your hand *is* power and might; in Your hand *it is* to make great and to give strength to all. Now therefore, our God, we thank You and praise Your glorious name.

3 Phil. 4:6, Be anxious for nothing, but in everything by prayer and supplication, with thanksgiving, let your requests be made known to God.

4 Rev. 22:20, He who testifies to these things says, "Surely I am coming quickly." Amen. Even so, come, Lord Jesus!

Comments

The "power of prayer" is not in ourselves – not in our spiritual-mindedness, our self-discipline, nor the fact that others are praying with us. Instead, it is in God Himself – who hears, who is pleased with His children drawing near to Him, and who is ever ready to grant their petitions, for Christ's sake (Dan. 9:23: Rom. 8:32; John 14:13; 15:16; 16:23-24). Praise and thanksgiving should be in our prayers often, without which our hearts quickly become stale and morbid from frequent repentance, petitions and intercessions.

When we say "Amen", meaning "So be it", do we actually believe that God will answer and, in fact, has answered in His own ways? We should be saying a hearty "Amen" whenever the person leading us ends his prayer (1 Cor. 14: 16). The "John Sung style" of prayer in which everyone prays at the same time, is not in accordance to the teaching of Scripture (1 Cor. 14:16 cf. vv. 27, 31). [This was

19. PRAYING FOR NEEDS

popularized by him, although not started by him. John Sung (1901-1944) was a famous evangelist from China who preached widely in Southeast Asia.]

Twenty

THE KINGDOM OF GOD

Q91.[1] How does God's kingdom extend on earth?
A91. God's kingdom extends by souls being brought under the rule of Christ[1-3], as the gospel is proclaimed to all nations[4-6], by His people who are gathered in visible and orderly churches[7-9].

1 Mark 1:14-15, Now after John was put in prison, Jesus came to Galilee, preaching the gospel of the kingdom of God, and saying, "The time is fulfilled, and the kingdom of God is at hand. Repent, and believe in the gospel."

2 Luke 17:20-21, Now when He was asked by the Pharisees when the kingdom of God would come, He answered them and said, "The kingdom of God does not come with observation; nor will they say, 'See here!' or 'See there!' For indeed, the kingdom of God is within you."

3 John 3:3, 5, Jesus answered and said to him, "Most assuredly, I say to you, unless one is born again, he cannot see the kingdom of God." ... Jesus answered, "Most assuredly, I say to you, unless

---

[1]This question connects with the previous one on the kingdom of God. It is added to inject a needed note on missions, which characterized the Particular Baptists of the 17th and 18th centuries, but missed out when they modeled their Catechism after the Westminster Shorter Catechism.

one is born of water and the Spirit, he cannot enter the kingdom of God."

4 Rom. 10:14-17, How then shall they call on Him in whom they have not believed? And how shall they believe in Him of whom they have not heard? And how shall they hear without a preacher? And how shall they preach unless they are sent? As it is written: *"How beautiful are the feet of those who preach the gospel of peace, who bring glad tidings of good things!"* But they have not all obeyed the gospel. For Isaiah says, *"LORD, who has believed our report?"* So then faith comes by hearing, and hearing by the word of God.

5 Luke 13:29, They will come from the east and the west, from the north and the south, and sit down in the kingdom of God.

6 Luke 16:16, The law and the prophets *were* until John. Since that time the kingdom of God has been preached, and everyone is pressing into it.

7 Matt. 28:18-20, And Jesus came and spoke to them, saying, "All authority has been given to Me in heaven and on earth. Go therefore and make disciples of all the nations, baptizing them in the name of the Father and of the Son and of the Holy Spirit, teaching them to observe all things that I have commanded you; and lo, I am with you always, *even* to the end of the age." Amen.

8 Luke 9:60, Jesus said to him, "Let the dead bury their own dead, but you go and preach the kingdom of God."

9 Acts 13:2-3, As they ministered to the Lord and fasted, the Holy Spirit said, "Now separate to Me Barnabas and Saul for the work to which I have called them." Then, having fasted and prayed, and laid hands on them, they sent *them* away.

Comments

The kingdom of God is not to be confused with any political entity or physical country. Rather, it is the rule of God in the hearts of men (Luke 17:21). It is the duty of individual Christians (Luke 9:60) and local churches (Rom. 10:15) to be involved in the Great Commission

20. THE KINGDOM OF GOD

of extending the kingdom of God (Matt. 28:18-20). Local church growth must go hand-in-hand with wider church planting (2 Cor. 10:15-16). The gospel must be brought to hearers, regardless of whether it is to one (John 4:7ff.; Acts 8:34-35; 9:11-12) or many (John 4:28-29, 39; 16:13), and whether publicly or from house to house (Acts 20:20-21). There should be persistence in preaching to the same people, until they are converted or the preachers are unwanted (Mark 6:6; Acts 19:8-10).

The gospel of "Jesus Christ and Him crucified" is to be preached from all the Scriptures (Luke 24:27, 44-45; 1 Pet. 1:23). It is the Lord's will that a living soul be the instrument to communicate spiritual life to those "dead in trespasses and sins" (Matt. 28:18-20; Eph. 2:1). Secondary helps such as tracts, books, Bible portions, radio, television, and the internet may be used, but not to supplant the physical presence of gospel preachers. Social concerns have their legitimate place, but not to the extent of supplanting the primary place of proclaiming the gospel (Matt. 5:13-14; Mark 14:7). Note that meeting social needs should begin with God's people (Rom. 15:26; Gal. 2:9-10; 6:10).

Q92.[2] What is the duty of those brought under the rule of Christ?
A92. Those brought under the rule of Christ are to seek baptism and be added to the membership of some visible and orderly church of Jesus Christ[1, 2], that they may walk in all the commandments and ordinances of the Lord blameless[3-5].

1 Matt. 28:18-20, And Jesus came and spoke to them, saying, "All authority has been given to Me in heaven and on earth. Go therefore and make disciples of all the nations, baptizing them in the name of the Father and of the Son and of the Holy Spirit, teaching them to observe all things that I have commanded you; and lo, I am with you always, *even* to the end of the age." Amen.

2 Acts 2:38, 41, 46-47, Then Peter said to them, "Repent, and let every one of you be baptized in the name of Jesus Christ for the remission of sins; and you shall receive the gift of the Holy Spirit." ...

---

[2]Keach's Catechism includes a similar question, retained by Spurgeon, on the duty of those baptized to become members of some visible church.

Then those who gladly received his word were baptized; and that day about three thousand souls were added *to them*. ... So continuing daily with one accord in the temple, and breaking bread from house to house, they ate their food with gladness and simplicity of heart, praising God and having favor with all the people. And the Lord added to the church daily those who were being saved.

3 Luke 1:6, And they were both righteous before God, walking in all the commandments and ordinances of the Lord blameless.

4 Matt. 7:21, "Not everyone who says to Me, 'Lord, Lord,' shall enter the kingdom of heaven, but he who does the will of My Father in heaven."

5 Heb. 10:24-25, And let us consider one another in order to stir up love and good works, not forsaking the assembling of ourselves together, as is the manner of some, but exhorting *one another*, and so much the more as you see the Day approaching.

Comments

Apart from exceptional situations (Acts 9:38-39), baptism involves being added to the membership of a local church (Matt. 28:18-20; Acts 2:41; 9:18-19). It is in the local church that one grows "in the grace and knowledge of our Lord and Saviour Jesus Christ" (2 Pet. 3:18; Matt. 28:20). The oneness of the local church as a body, and as a temple, cannot be fully applied to those who are not members (1 Cor. 12:25-26; 1 Pet. 2:5). Similarly, the teaching on church discipline and service to God cannot be properly applied to non-members (1 Cor. 5:12; Rom. 12:1).

It is the duty of all believers to be members of some local church somewhere. Membership involves privileges and responsibilities, consistent with those who are bound together by the church covenant (see Q93). A church member should not think only of what he may gain out of the church, but how he may contribute to the building up of the church (1 Cor. 10:23-24; 12:7). The local church is central and unique in the purposes of God (Matt. 28:18-20; Acts 13:1-3; 14:23, 26; Rev. 1:12-13, 20). Service to God should be in, and through, the local church primarily. We should be like Zacharias and

20. THE KINGDOM OF GOD

Elizabeth, "righteous before God, walking in all the commandments and ordinances of the Lord blameless" (Luke 1:6).

Q93.[3] What is the visible church?
A93. The visible church is the organized society of baptized believers who are bound to one another and to the Lord by voluntary covenant[1-3], to worship God and to serve the Lord Jesus Christ in accordance to the Scripture[4-7].

1 1 Cor. 12:12, For as the body is one and has many members, but all the members of that one body, being many, are one body, so also *is* Christ.

2 2 Cor. 7:3, I do not say *this* to condemn; for I have said before that you are in our hearts, to die together and to live together.

3 2 Cor. 8:5, And not *only* as we had hoped, but they first gave themselves to the Lord, and *then* to us by the will of God.

4 Matt. 28:18-20, And Jesus came and spoke to them, saying, "All authority has been given to Me in heaven and on earth. Go therefore and make disciples of all the nations, baptizing them in the name of the Father and of the Son and of the Holy Spirit, teaching them to observe all things that I have commanded you; and lo, I am with you always, *even* to the end of the age." Amen.

5 Acts 2:42, And they continued steadfastly in the apostles' doctrine and fellowship, in the breaking of bread, and in prayers.

6 Acts 20:7, Now on the first *day* of the week, when the disciples came together to break bread, Paul, ready to depart the next day, spoke to them and continued his message until midnight.

7 Eph. 4:11-12, And He Himself gave some *to be* apostles, some prophets, some evangelists, and some pastors and teachers, for the equipping of the saints for the work of ministry, for the edifying of the body of Christ.

---

[3]Keach's Catechism includes the question on the visible church, left out by Spurgeon, which we have thoroughly revised and split into two.

Comments

The *matter* (or members), *form* (or constitution), and *function* (or purpose) together define the local church. The local church is "visible" because the members may be known, in contrast to those who are not members (1 Cor. 14:23-24). In other words, there is an explicit membership, distinguishing those who are members of the church from those who are attending the congregation only. Admission to membership is by baptism (Acts 2:41). Baptized believers coming from other churches may apply for membership. The church covenant gives form to the local church. The church exists to worship, and to serve, God in accordance to the teaching of the Bible.

The idea of the church being an organized society has been rejected by many professing believers in the past and at the present, often under the pretext of holding to the principles of "the priesthood of all believers" and "the voluntary nature of discipleship". The principle of "the priesthood of all believers" (1 Pet. 1:9-10; Heb. 10:19-22) means that every believer may worship God without the need of human mediation. It is no license for us to do as we like (Rom. 6:18). Instead, it carries the implication that we must serve God in His way (1 Cor. 14:26, 40). The principle of "the voluntary nature of discipleship" (Luke 9:49-50; Rom. 14:7-8, 12-13) means that we are not forced against our will to be saved. Instead, we are regenerated by the grace of God to come willingly to Christ. This principle is no license for us to hold back from doing what is right, good and true (2 Chron. 31:20-21; 1 Cor. 12:15-16, 20-21). Rather, it requires that we serve God willingly, out of love for Him (Mal. 3:17; Luke 1:74; Rom. 12:1-2; Heb. 9:14).

Q94. What are the marks by which a true church may be recognized?
A94. A true church may be recognized by the marks of the gospel being truly preached[1], the special ordinances of baptism and the Lord's Supper being rightly administered[2,3], and church discipline being correctly practised[4-6].

20. THE KINGDOM OF GOD

1 Gal. 1:8-9, But even if we, or an angel from heaven, preach any other gospel to you than what we have preached to you, let him be accursed. As we have said before, so now I say again, if anyone preaches any other gospel to you than what you have received, let him be accursed.

2 Matt. 28:18-20, And Jesus came and spoke to them, saying, "All authority has been given to Me in heaven and on earth. Go therefore and make disciples of all the nations, baptizing them in the name of the Father and of the Son and of the Holy Spirit, teaching them to observe all things that I have commanded you; and lo, I am with you always, *even* to the end of the age." Amen.

3 1 Cor. 11:23, 26-27, For I received from the Lord that which I also delivered to you: that the Lord Jesus on the *same* night in which He was betrayed took bread. ... For as often as you eat this bread and drink this cup, you proclaim the Lord's death till He comes. Therefore whoever eats this bread or drinks *this* cup of the Lord in an unworthy manner will be guilty of the body and blood of the Lord.

4 1 Thess. 5:12-13, And we urge you, brethren, to recognize those who labor among you, and are over you in the Lord and admonish you, and to esteem them very highly in love for their work's sake. Be at peace among yourselves.

5 2 Thess. 3:6, 14-15, But we command you, brethren, in the name of our Lord Jesus Christ, that you withdraw from every brother who walks disorderly and not according to the tradition which he received from us. ... And if anyone does not obey our word in this epistle, note that person and do not keep company with him, that he may be ashamed. Yet do not count *him* as an enemy, but admonish *him* as a brother.

6 1 Cor. 5:4-5, 12, In the name of our Lord Jesus Christ, when you are gathered together, along with my spirit, with the power of our Lord Jesus Christ, deliver such a one to Satan for the destruction of the flesh, that his spirit may be saved in the day of the Lord Jesus. ... For what *have* I *to do* with judging those also who are outside? Do you not judge those who are inside?

Comments

A church can go astray imperceptibly, reaching a point at which it cannot be regarded as a true church any more (cf. Rev. 2:12-16). A church that preaches a perverted gospel (Gal. 1:6-9), or distorts the Lord's Supper, as happens in the Roman Catholic Church, cannot be regarded as a true one. A church that is too lax (cf. 1 Cor. 5:1-2, 12-13), or too rigid (cf. 3 John 9-10), in discipline is in danger of becoming a false church. The Bible teaches three levels of discipline – admonition (1 Thess. 5:12-13; Tit. 1:13; 3:10), suspension (2 Thess. 3:6, 14-15) and excommunication (1 Cor. 5:4-5). The purpose of discipline is primarily to restore the sinning brother (Gal. 6:1), although it has a secondary deterrent effect (1 Tim. 5:20).

The degree of fellowship between churches is determined by the amount of truth held in common. The more truth is held in common, the greater is the possibility of fellowship. Some truths are fundamental to the Christian faith, while others are not so critical (Gal. 1:6-9; Heb. 6:1-3; 2 John 7). Doctrine cannot be separated from practice. Doctrine leads to practice, and practice is based on doctrine. Separation from those who are in serious error – whether in doctrine or in practice – is taught in the Bible (Rom. 16:17-18; 2 Thess. 3:14-15; 2 John 10). A believer should seek out a good church to be a member there. Unity is to be pursued *in the truth* (Eph. 4:4-6), and in the *spirit* of the truth (Eph. 4:1-3). A church can be hard and harsh while proclaiming and upholding the truth. There may be a zeal that is without love, an orthodoxy that is devoid of humanity.

Q95. Why are these marks essential?
A95. These marks are essential as they arise from the recognition of Jesus Christ as the only foundation of the church[1-3], and its only head[4], who occupies the offices of prophet[5, 6], priest[7], and king[8].

1 1 Cor. 3:11, For no other foundation can anyone lay than that which is laid, which is Jesus Christ.

20. THE KINGDOM OF GOD

2 Matt. 16:15-18, He said to them, "But who do you say that I am?" Simon Peter answered and said, "You are the Christ, the Son of the living God." Jesus answered and said to him, "Blessed are you, Simon Bar-Jonah, for flesh and blood has not revealed *this* to you, but My Father who is in heaven. And I also say to you that you are Peter, and on this rock I will build My church, and the gates of Hades shall not prevail against it."

3 Eph. 2:19-22, Now, therefore, you are no longer strangers and foreigners, but fellow citizens with the saints and members of the household of God, having been built on the foundation of the apostles and prophets, Jesus Christ Himself being the chief corner*stone*, in whom the whole building, being fitted together, grows into a holy temple in the Lord, in whom you also are being built together for a dwelling place of God in the Spirit.

4 Col. 1:18, And He is the head of the body, the church, who is the beginning, the firstborn from the dead, that in all things He may have the preeminence.

5 John 4:19, The woman said to Him, "Sir, I perceive that You are a prophet."

6 Acts 3:22, For Moses truly said to the Fathers, *'The LORD your God will raise up for you a Prophet like me from your brethren. Him you shall hear in all things, whatever He says to you.'*

7 Heb. 9:11, But Christ came *as* High Priest of the good things to come, with the greater and more perfect tabernacle not made with hands, that is, not of this creation.

8 Rev. 19:16, And He has on *His* robe and on His thigh a name written: KING OF KINGS AND LORD OF LORDS.

Comments

As the Mediator between God and man, and as the Head of the church, Jesus Christ occupies the offices of prophet, priest and king. The church that truly submits to Christ as Head would show submission to Him in His three offices – in doctrine, worship, and church government. At the barest minimum, a true church would show these three marks – the preaching of the true gospel, the right administration of the special ordinances, and biblical church discipline.

A church differs from other organizations in that it has Christ alone as its foundation, and Christ alone as its Head. Without Christ, the church would be no different from other organizations, in essence and in purpose. Just as an individual grows in holiness and spirituality (2 Pet. 3:18), so also the church should grow (Eph. 5:27). Wrongs must be put right (e.g. 1 Cor. 5:2; Rev. 2:12-16), while the truth must be pursued (1 Cor. 3:9-15; Heb. 6:1-3). In the work of reforming the church, the number and order of Christ's offices should be adhered to. Begin by reforming the doctrine of the church, then the worship, and finally the form of church government.

Q96. Is there a recognizable form of church government taught in the Bible?
A96. The Bible teaches a recognizable form of church government[1,2] called Independency[3-5], which is different from Episcopacy, Presbyterianism, and Congregationalism.

1. 1 Tim. 3:15, But if I am delayed, *I write* so that you may know how you ought to conduct yourself in the house of God, which is the church of the living God, the pillar and ground of the truth.

2. Tit. 1:5, For this reason I left you in Crete, that you should set in order the things that are lacking, and appoint elders in every city as I commanded you—

3. Matt. 18:17, And if he refuses to hear them, tell it to the church. But if he refuses even to hear the church, let him be to you like a heathen and a tax collector.

4. Acts 14:23, So when they had appointed elders in every church, and prayed with fasting, they commended them to the Lord in whom they had believed.

5. Rev. 1:12, 13, 20, Then I turned to see the voice that spoke with me. And having turned I saw seven golden lampstands, and in the midst of the seven lampstands *One* like the Son of Man, clothed

with a garment down to the feet and girded about the chest with a golden band. The mystery of the seven stars which you saw in My right hand, and the seven golden lampstands: The seven stars are the angels of the seven churches, and the seven lampstands which you saw are the seven churches.

Comments

Historically, four basic forms of church government are recognizable. In **Episcopacy**, there is a hierarchy of individuals who exercise power over many local congregations. The Church of England and many Methodist denominations practise this. In **Presbyterianism**, the hierarchy is in committees of individuals who have the power over many congregations. **Independency** and **Congregationalism** hold to the autonomy of the local church. However, the manner of exercising rule differs in the two. In Congregationalism, the power and the execution of rule are regarded as given by Christ to the congregation. Decisions are made by discussion in the congregation followed by voting to determine the will of the majority. In Independency, the power of rule resides with the congregation but the authority to execute the rule lies with the elders. The elders lead in making decisions, which are put to the congregation for its consent.

Para-church organizations exist, purportedly, to complement the work of churches, and even to help churches. They exist for certain limited objectives, e.g. to send out missionaries, to reach out to campus students, to publish Christian literature, etc. The membership of such organizations is drawn from people of various churches. Normally, the special ordinances of baptism and the Lord's Supper are not carried out, as they rightly realize that these ordinances do not belong to their domain. Furthermore, these organizations are not administered according to any form of church government but follow pragmatic approaches of administration akin to secular organizations. While acknowledging the good accomplished by many of such organizations, Christians should understand that these are not churches. Involvement with such organizations should not supplant their commitment to a good local church.

Q97. What are the characteristics of Independency?
A97. Independency upholds the headship of Christ[1], the autonomy of the local church[2], the priority of the ministry[3], rule by elders[4], and rule with congregational consent[5].

1. Col. 1:18, And He is the head of the body, the church, who is the beginning, the firstborn from the dead, that in all things He may have the preeminence.

2. Matt. 18:17, And if he refuses to hear them, tell it to the church. But if he refuses even to hear the church, let him be to you like a heathen and a tax collector.

3. 1 Tim. 5:17, Let the elders who rule well be counted worthy of double honor, especially those who labor in the word and doctrine.

4. Heb. 13:17, Obey those who rule over you, and be submissive, for they watch out for your souls, as those who must give account. Let them do so with joy and not with grief, for that would be unprofitable for you.

5. 1 Cor. 5:4-5, In the name of our Lord Jesus Christ, when you are gathered together, along with my spirit, with the power of our Lord Jesus Christ, deliver such a one to Satan for the destruction of the flesh, that his spirit may be saved in the day of the Lord Jesus.

Comments

The doctrine of "sola scriptura" states that the Bible is the only authority in all matters of faith and practice (2 Tim. 3:16-17). Through the centuries, God's people struggled to understand and apply the Bible's teaching to the governance of the church. This gave rise to the four basic forms of church government that have come down to us historically. We believe that Independency is the form of church government taught in the Bible because all its chief characteristics are biblical, namely, (i) upholding consistently the headship of Christ; (ii) the church being self-ruled, (iii) the leading role of the teaching elder, (iv) rule is exercised by the elders; and (v) the necessity of congregational consent in decision-making. There are those who hold to the idea that "all pastors are elders, and all elders are pastors". They deny the validity of ruling elders who help the teaching elder (or pastor) in governing the church. Theirs is a distorted form of Independency.

It is possible to be a true church, and even a good church, while practising a form of church government other than Independency. On the other hand, a church may have the right form of church government but falls far short of the Bible's teaching in other areas. Many churches today attempt to incorporate the methods and structures of business management in the governance of the church, while maintaining a semblance of adherence to the Bible by retaining the titles of "pastor", "elders" and "deacons". At the root of such innovation is failure to uphold the doctrine of "sola scriptura".

Q98.[4] What is the invisible church?
A98. The invisible church is the whole number of the elect, that have been, are, or shall be gathered into one under Christ as head[1-4].

1 Eph. 1:10, 22-23, That in the dispensation of the fullness of the times He might gather together in one all things in Christ, both which are in heaven and which are on earth—in Him. ... And He put all *things* under His feet, and gave Him *to be* head over all *things* to the church, which is His body, the fullness of Him who fills all in all.

2 Eph. 5:25-27, Husbands, love your wives, just as Christ also loved the church and gave Himself for her, that He might sanctify and cleanse her with the washing of water by the word, that He might present her to Himself a glorious church, not having spot or wrinkle or any such thing, but that she should be holy and without blemish.

---

[4]This is from Keach's Catechism, which was left out by Spurgeon.

3 John 10:16, And other sheep I have which are not of this fold; them also I must bring, and they will hear My voice; and there will be one flock *and* one shepherd.

4 John 11:52, And not for that nation only, but also that He would gather together in one the children of God who were scattered abroad.

Comments

Landmarkism (after the title of a book), which is taught by some Baptists, denies the existence of the invisible, or universal, church. Its other peculiarities include the non-recognition of those who are not Baptists, the practice of close-communion (i.e. limiting the Lord's Supper to members of the local church), the rejection of alien immersion (i.e. immersion not authorized by a certain type of Baptist churches), and adherence to the theory of church succession through believer's baptism. Paedobaptists (including the Anglican, Presbyterian and Methodist Churches) believe in a "visible universal church", consisting of believers and their children, who are "baptized" by sprinkling. They also practise some forms of hierarchical church government which have authority beyond the local church.

We believe that the universal church is invisible in the sense that the work of grace in the lives of believers cannot be seen. Furthermore, it is practically impossible for us to know all believers in heaven, on earth, and those who will be saved in the future. The universal church may be regarded as consisting of *the church triumphant* (i.e. of believers already in heaven) and *the church militant* (i.e. of believers who are on earth). The universal church manifests itself in the world as visible local churches. Entry into the universal church is by the regeneration of the Holy Spirit (John 3:3, 5), while membership in the local church is by baptism (Acts 2:41).

Q99.[5] What will become of the kingdom of God?
A99. The kingdom of God will reach its climax in God's plan with the salvation of all God's elect[1-3], the punishment of the

20. THE KINGDOM OF GOD

wicked[4, 5], the transformation of all creation[6-8], and the everlasting reign of Christ in the new heavens and new earth, subject to the Father, in full trinitarian glory[9-11].

1 Matt. 24:31, And He will send His angels with a great sound of a trumpet, and they will gather together His elect from the four winds, from one end of heaven to the other.

2 John 10:16, 28, And other sheep I have which are not of this fold; them also I must bring, and they will hear My voice; and there will be one flock and one shepherd. ... And I give them eternal life, and they shall never perish; neither shall anyone snatch them out of My hand.

3 Rom. 8:38-39, For I am persuaded that neither death nor life, nor angels nor principalities nor powers, nor things present nor things to come, nor height nor depth, nor any other created thing, shall be able to separate us from the love of God which is in Christ Jesus our Lord.

4 Matt. 13:41-43, The Son of Man will send out His angels, and they will gather out of His kingdom all things that offend, and those who practice lawlessness, and will cast them into the furnace of fire. There will be wailing and gnashing of teeth. Then the righteous will shine forth as the sun in the kingdom of their Father. He who has ears to hear, let him hear!

5 Matt. 24:50-51, The master of that servant will come on a day when he is not looking for *him* and at an hour that he is not aware of, and will cut him in two and appoint *him* his portion with the hypocrites. There shall be weeping and gnashing of teeth.

6 2 Pet. 3:10, 13, But the day of the Lord will come as a thief in the night, in which the heavens will pass away with a great noise, and the elements will melt with fervent heat; both the earth and the works that are in it will be burned up. ... Nevertheless we, according to His promise, look for new heavens and a new earth in which righteousness dwells.

---

[5]This is added to our Catechism for completeness.

7 Rom. 8:21, Because the creation itself also will be delivered from the bondage of corruption into the glorious liberty of the children of God.

8 Rev. 21:1, 4, Now I saw a new heaven and a new earth, for the first heaven and the first earth had passed away. Also there was no more sea. ... And God will wipe away every tear from their eyes; there shall be no more death, nor sorrow, nor crying. There shall be no more pain, for the former things have passed away.

9 1 Cor. 15:28, Now when all things are made subject to Him, then the Son Himself will also be subject to Him who put all things under Him, that God may be all in all.

10 Eph. 1:22-23, And He put all *things* under His feet, and gave Him *to be* head over all *things* to the church, which is His body, the fullness of Him who fills all in all.

11 Rev. 22:1-3, And he showed me a pure river of water of life, clear as crystal, proceeding from the throne of God and of the Lamb. In the middle of its street, and on either side of the river, *was* the tree of life, which bore twelve fruits, each *tree* yielding its fruit every month. The leaves of the tree *were* for the healing of the nations. And there shall be no more curse, but the throne of God and of the Lamb shall be in it, and His servants shall serve Him.

Comments

According to the Greek worldview, there are three heavens (cf. 2 Pet. 3:13) – the air around us being the first, the outer space being the second, and the dwelling place of God being the third (2 Cor. 12:2). Heaven, the dwelling place of God, is already perfect and cannot be improved upon qualitatively. However, it is not complete in the sense that not all the elect are gathered together yet. When that happens, heaven will incorporate the renewed physical universe. In other words, the earth and all the celestial bodies will be melted down and made new, and become part of the new heaven. Earth will be in heaven, and heaven will be on earth (Rev. 21:1-3).

Upon the return of Christ, all the dead will be raised and judged together with the living (Matt. 25:31-33). The wicked will be cast

20. THE KINGDOM OF GOD

into the eternal suffering of hell in their inglorious bodies, which is the second death (Rev. 20:14). The place of eternal torment for the wicked will not be part of the new heaven (Rev. 21:8). The righteous will dwell with the Lord in their glorified bodies on the new earth, which is part of the new heaven. Sin and its effects will no longer trouble God's people (Rev. 21:4). God's people will serve the Lord and worship Him perfectly (Rev. 7:15; 22:3). The Lord Jesus Christ will reign for ever, in full trinitarian glory. To the trinitarian God we sing, "For of Him and through Him and to Him *are* all things, to whom *be* glory forever. Amen (Rom. 11:36)."

INDEX

Abraham, 37, 69, 92, 118, 136
Adam, 18, 21, 24-27, 36, 68, 96, 25n
addition, 46, 102
admonition, 150
adoption, 51-56
adultery, 86-88
affinity, 88
Agnosticism, 10
Ahab, 63
Alpha Course, ix
Amen, x, 139, 140, 159
Amyraldianism, 33
Amyraut, Moses, 33
Annihilationism, 29, 64
anthropomorphism, 10
anti-type, 120
Antinomianism, 70, 96
antithetical, 132
Apocrypha, 5
Appollinarians, 36
Arians, 35
Arminianism, 24, 33, 103
Arminius, James, 33
ascension, 43
asceticism, 18
Atheism, 10
attributes, 10, 18, 77
autonomy, 153, 154
baptism, xi, xiii, xiv, 46, 53, 70, 102, 106, 109, 110, 112, 113, 118-123, 145, 146, 148, 153, 156, 117n, 118n
   infant b., 120
Baptists, xiii, 113, 156
   General B., xiii

Particular B., x, xiii, 143n
Reformed B., ix, xiii, xiv
Barthianism, 4, 5
Baxter, Richard, 34
Body of Divinity, xiii
bread, 76, 122-124, 135, 136
burial, 60, 117, 118, 121
Campbell, Alexander, 106
Campbellites, 70
Catechism, ix, x, xiv, 73n, 75n, 77n, 79n, 83n, 93n, 110n, 143n, 157n
   Children's C., xiv
   Keach's C., x, xiii, xiv, 113, 63n, 103n, 145n, 147n, 155n
   RC C., 113
   Shorter C., 103n
   Shorter C. Baptist Version, xiv
   Spurgeon's C, xiv, 127n
   Westminster Shorter C., xiii, 143n
catechism(s), ix, xi-xiv, 6, 7, 12
chance, 15, 16, 29
catechism(s), 6, 7, 12
chance, 15, 16, 29
Charismatic movement, 12, 54, 53n
Christian Reconstructionism, 132
Church(es)
   C. of Christ, 70, 106
   C. of England, ix, xiii, 153
   Anglican C., ix, 156
   Brethren C., ix, xii
   Evangelical Free C., ix, xii
   Lutheran C., 70
   Methodist C., ix, xii, 156
   Orthodox C., xi

Presbyterian C., 156
Roman Catholic C., xi, xii, 5, 36, 53, 70, 76, 96, 97, 113, 125, 150
church, 84, 85
    church militant, 156
    church triumphant, 156
    confessional c., ix, xii
    form of c., 148
    function of c., 148
    invisible c., 155
    local c., 112, 113, 145, 146, 148, 153, 154, 156
    matter of c., 148
    universal c., 156
    visible c., 145, 147, 156
circumcision, 118, 120
Collins, William, xiii
communion, 28, 115
    close-c., 156
    closed c., 125
    open c., 125
    restricted c., 125
Confession of Faith
    1689 C., xiii, 34
    Westminster C., xiii
confession(s) of faith, ix, xii, xiii, 7, 39
confirmation, 113
Congregationalism, 153
Congregationalists, xiii
consanguinity, 88
conscience, 56, 67
consubstantiation, 125
Council of Chalcedon, 36
covenant, 21, 53, 120, 147, 25n
    c. of grace, 31, 32, 120
    c. of works, 20, 21, 32
    church c., 146, 148
    marriage c., 88
    new c., 118, 120, 122
    old c., 71
covetousness, 70, 94
creation, 16-18, 32, 54, 67, 87, 96, 131, 157
    gap theory of c., 17, 18
    process c., 17

progressive c., 17
Creed,
    Apostles' C., xii
    Athanasian C., xii
    Chalcedonian C., 36
    Nicene C., xii
creed(s), ix, xii
cremation, 60
cup, 122-124, 122n
Daniel, 115
Darwinism, 17
David, 25, 37
deacons, 155
dichotomy, 60
discipline, 41, 84, 112, 114, 115, 125, 131, 146, 148, 150, 152
distortion, 46, 102
divorce, 88
Docetists, 35
ecumenical councils, xii
elder(s), 84, 152-155
Elizabeth, 147
Episcopacy, 153
Esau, 63
eschatological, 132
Eunomians, 35
Eve, 24-27, 96
evolution, 24
    atheistic e., 17
    theistic e., 17
    theory of e., 16, 17
excommunication, 150
expediency, 5
extreme unction, 113
faith, ix, xi, xii, xiv, 4-7, 11, 34, 46-48, 52, 53, 55-57, 62, 68-70, 74, 78, 92, 102-106, 109, 110, 112, 118-120, 122, 124, 128, 130, 138, 154, 102n
    Christian f., ix, xi, xiv, 150
    credible profession of f., 119
Fall, 21, 24-26, 29, 32, 68, 96, 95n
fasting, 110, 115
fatalism, 94
fate, 15, 16
feminist movement, 20

INDEX

forgiveness, 96, 137, 138
fornication, 87
free offer of the gospel, 49, 104, 47n
fruit of the vine, 123
Fuller, Andrew, 34
Gnosticism, 18, 61
good works, 55
gospel, xiv, 6, 33, 39, 41, 47, 48, 86, 90, 101-105, 112, 113, 119, 122, 132, 143, 145, 150, 152
government, xiii, 84, 86, 90, 131
    church g., x, xiii, 41, 152-156
grace, xiv, 12, 52, 53, 55, 56, 62, 68-70, 87, 97, 106, 113, 119, 122, 128, 130-133, 136, 139, 146, 148, 156
    common g., 106
    means of g., 109
    saving g., 104-106
Great Commission, 49, 132, 144
head, 26, 39, 84, 150-152, 155
headship, 38, 154
healing, 13, 110
heart, 26, 38, 68-70, 94, 105, 125, 128, 137, 19n, 47n, 133n
heaven, 3, 25, 40, 43, 60-62, 64, 75, 76, 92, 94, 96, 97, 129, 130, 132, 133, 156, 158, 159
hell, 28, 29, 62-64, 97, 159
Herod Agrippa I, 41
High Priest, 40, 130
higher life, 56, 96
Hyper-Calvinism, 103
immersion, 114, 121, 156
    alien i., 156
imputation, 53
Independency, 153-155
infusion, 53
intermediate state, 60
Invincible Grace, 46
irresistible, 46
Iscariot, Judas, 63, 105
Israel, 25, 40, 68, 69
Jehovah's Witnesses, 34, 74
Jeroboam son of Nebat, 63
Jezebel, 63

judgement, xiii, 21, 29, 53, 60-63, 86, 98, 61n
justification, 51-56, 137
    j. by faith, 53, 55, 56, 106
    eternal j., 53
Keach, Benjamin, xiii
kenosis theory, 42
Keswick Convention, 56
king, 20, 37, 40, 76, 84, 150, 151, 19n
kingdom of God, x, 132, 133, 136, 143-145, 157, 143n
kingship, 41
Landmarkism, 156
law, xiii, xiv, 6, 24-28, 32, 41, 42, 68, 70, 71, 94-98
    ceremonial l., 69
    civil l., 69
    First Table of the L., 70
    moral l., 67-70
    Second Table of the L., 70
Lazarus, 47
legalism, 124
Liberalism, 4, 5, 24
litotes, 138
Lord's Prayer, xiii, 129, 139, 127n
Lord's Supper, 81, 109, 110, 112-114, 122-125, 148, 150, 153, 156
luck, 15, 16
Luther, Martin, xii, 53
marriage, 36, 62, 70, 78, 87, 88
mass, 46, 53, 70, 102, 106, 113
matrimony, 113
maximalism, 102
means of grace, 56, 57, 110, 115, 133, 139, 103n
Mediator, 37, 130, 151
meditation, 112, 115, 109n
Melchizedek, 40
membership, 131, 145, 146, 148, 153, 156
Methodist, 56, 153
mind, 26, 38, 69, 105, 125, 19n, 47n, 133n,
minimalism, 102
miracles, 36, 110
Modernism, 36

Modernists, 24, 46, 102
Moses, 37
Mother of God, 36
Nebuchadnezzar, 136
Neo-orthodoxy, 5
New Covenant Theology, 70
New Perspectives on Paul, 53
Normative Principle, 76
offices, 37, 38, 41, 150-152
ordinances, 75, 77, 110, 113, 123, 145, 147
   holy o., 113
   special o., 110, 113, 117, 118, 122, 148, 152, 153
ordination, 113
orthodoxy, 150
paedobaptist(s), 118, 120, 125, 156
pagan(s), xiv, 74, 76, 119, 128
paganism, 74
para-church organizations, 153
Parable of the Sower, 48
pastor(s), 155
Paul, xi, 24, 80, 94, 102
penance, 106, 113
Perfectionism, 56, 96
Permissive Principle, 76
Perseverance of the Saints, 57
Pharisees, 115, 124
pouring, 122
pragmatism, 5
prayer, 40, 57, 76, 81, 109, 110, 113-115, 118, 127-130, 135, 139, 140
pre-Adamic man, 18
Presbyterianism, 153
priest, 20, 37, 39, 46, 102, 150, 151, 19n
priesthood, 40, 41
   p. of all believers, 148
prophecy, 54
prophet, 20, 37-39, 150, 151, 19n
prophethood, 41
Protestant, xii, 6
providence, 16, 18, 20
purgatory, 60, 97
reconciliation, 106, 137
Redeemer, 31-34, 37

Reformation, ix, xii, 5, 53, 113
regeneration, 12, 120, 132, 156
Regulative Principle, 76
relative, 25
repentance, xiv, 6, 46, 47, 102-106, 110, 118, 124, 125, 137, 140, 102n, 103n
resurrection, 38, 43, 59, 60, 62, 79, 117, 118, 121, 61n
revelation, 5, 10, 39
   natural r., 67
   special r., 67
righteousness, 19, 32, 42, 52, 53, 55, 94, 98, 106, 115, 118, 120, 133, 19n, 27n
rosary, 128
Sabbath, 71, 78-80
saints, 96
salvation, xiv, 6, 7, 31, 33, 37-39, 45, 48, 49, 51, 53, 54, 59, 62, 67, 69, 70, 74, 96, 101-103, 105, 106, 110, 112, 118, 119, 132, 137, 156, 38n, 47n, 101n
sanctification, 12, 51, 52, 54-56, 70, 137
   entire s., 56
sanctity of lawful authorities, 70, 84
sanctity of life, 86
sanctity of marriage, 87
sanctity of private property, 90
sanctity of speech, 92
sanctity of the heart, 94
Saul, 41, 103
Savoy Declaration, xiii
seal, 118
second death, 64, 159 *semper reformanda*, ix
separation, 131, 150
sign, 117, 118, 120, 122
sins of omission, 24
sola scriptura, ix, 5, 154, 155
soul sleep, 60
sovereignty of God, 103, 136
sprinkling, 120, 122, 156
Spurgeon, C. H., x, xiii, 17, 23n, 55n, 61n, 68n, 73n, 77n, 95n,

104n, 105n, 109n, 110n, 117n, 145n, 147n, 155n
subjective, 25
subtraction, 46, 102
Sung, John, 140, 141
suspension, 150
syncretism, 74
temptation, 56, 138, 139
Ten Commandments, xiii, 24, 68-71, 73n
Theonomy movement, 132
Theophilus, xi
Thirty-nine Articles, ix
tongue-speaking, 12, 110
Total Depravity, 28
traditions, 5
transubstantiation, 125
trichotomy, 60
trinitarian, 74, 107, 127, 157, 159
type, 120, 123
Unconditional Election, 32
unity, xii, 150
Universal Atonement, 33
victorious life, 55
virgin birth, 36
voluntary nature of discipleship, 148
water, 5, 75, 121, 122
Watson, Thomas, xiii
will, 26, 105, 125, 153, 19n, 47n, 133n
    free w., 21, 23, 24
    God's w., 3, 5, 6, 15, 19, 38, 67, 68, 127, 128, 132, 133, 138, 145-147, 38n
    man's w., 15, 24, 47, 148
wine, 123, 122n
worship, 11, 20, 40, 69, 70, 73-76, 78-81, 128, 131, 147, 148, 152, 159
Zacharias, 146

www.ingramcontent.com/pod-product-compliance
Lightning Source LLC
Chambersburg PA
CBHW071503040426
42444CB00008B/1467